Terrorism,
the Laws of War
and the Constitution

Terrorism, the Laws of War, and the Constitution

Debating the Enemy Combatant Cases

Edited by
Peter Berkowitz

HOOVER INSTITUTION PRESS
Stanford University   Stanford, California

www.hoover.org

Hoover Institution Press Publication No. 537

First printing, 2005
12   11   10   09   08   07   9   8   7   6   5   4   3   2

Manufactured in the United States of America

The paper used in this publication meets the minimum requirements
of the American National Standard for Information Sciences—
Permanence of Paper for Printed Library Materials, ANSI Z39.48-1992. ∞

Library of Congress Cataloging-in-Publication Data
Terrorism, the laws of war, and the Constitution : debating the enemy
combatant cases / edited by Peter Berkowitz.
      p.   cm. — (Hoover Institution Press publication series ; 537)
   Includes bibliographical references and index.
   ISBN 0-8179-4622-5 (alk. paper)
   1. Combatants and noncombatants—Legal status, laws, etc.—United
States.   2. War (International law)   3. Constitutional law—United States.
4. Detention of persons—United States.   5. Terrorism—United States.
6. War on Terrorism, 2001–   7. National security—United States.
I. Berkowitz, Peter, 1959–   II. Series: Hoover Institution Press
publication ; 537.
KF7225.T48   2005
343.73'01—dc22   2005003039

Contents

Acknowledgments

The editor is grateful to Jack Goldsmith, who provided valuable comments on several of the chapters, as well as on the Introduction. And it is a pleasure to again thank Hoover Institution director John Raisian and deputy director David Brady for their support.

* * *

The Hoover Institution wishes to acknowledge the generous support of the McCormick Tribune Foundation that made this book possible.

The Institution also wishes to thank supporters of the initiative on National Priorities, International Rivalries, and Global Cooperation, including the Bradley Foundation and Jeronimo and Javier Arango.

Introduction

Peter Berkowitz

AL QAEDA'S SEPTEMBER 11 attack on the United States marked the advent of a new era of warfare. Until that awful day, the dominant view held that only a state could threaten another state's political sovereignty or territorial integrity. But the destruction of the World Trade Center Towers, the assault on the Pentagon, the attempted strike on the Capitol Building or the White House thwarted by the heroic passengers of flight 91, and the murder of more than 3,000 innocent civilians demonstrated that the dominant view was inadequate. Modern technology had placed in the hands of nonstate actors—shadowy terrorist networks and bands of fanatical thugs—the power to bring a state to its knees.

Like all wars, the global war on terror proclaimed by the Bush administration—or better, the U.S.-led worldwide war against Islamic extremists whose weapon of choice is terror—has put strain on the rule of law. This is in part because of the ways in which American constitutional law is entangled with the modern laws of war and their long-standing assumption that the principal actors in war are states. The modern laws of war are a part of the law of nations that emerged in the writings of seventeenth- and eighteenth-century jurists and political thinkers and that developed in accordance with the evolving practices of modern nation states. In the aftermath of World War II and the founding of the United Nations, those laws have been a subject of increasingly intense interest and elaboration by international human rights lawyers. Specifying the rights and duties laid down by the laws of war can be difficult, because the laws of war stem from diverse sources—treaties, customary state practice, and abstract speculation. But the main cause of difficulty today is that the laws of war were developed with a particular conception of war in mind—involving states with incentives to engage in reciprocal restraint—that does not apply to the conflict with the United States' new adversaries. To further complicate matters, although American jurists generally agree that the laws of war are pertinent under the Constitution, they disagree vigorously on how those laws apply. Still, the central challenge for American constitutional law in the war on terror, as for the laws of war more generally, arises from the nature of a new kind of adversary who controls no territory, defends no settled population, hides among and targets noncombatant civilian populations, and seeks to acquire and use weapons of mass destruction.

In spring 2004, the first set of challenges under the Constitution made its way to the U.S. Supreme Court. These challenges came in the form of three cases concerning the process due to detainees who the United States holds as enemy combatants—those who take up arms and wage war against the United States. All invoked the writ of habeas corpus, the venerable legal means by which a prisoner asks a court to review the legality of his detention. In *Rumsfeld v. Padilla* (124 S. Ct. 2711 [2004]), the least consequential, the Court declined to consider the merits of the case. Jose Padilla, a U.S. citizen arrested in Chicago in May 2002 on suspicion of involvement in an al Qaeda plot to detonate a "dirty bomb" in the United States, had been held as an enemy combatant in a military brig in South Carolina without charges, without trial, and without access to a lawyer. In a lawsuit filed in the Southern District—which includes New York, where

Padilla was initially detained in federal criminal custody—Padilla contended that in detaining him, the government had violated his constitutional rights. The government responded that the war powers entrusted by the Constitution to the executive branch permitted the president to designate Padilla as an enemy combatant and that such designation overrode the rights to criminal due process that Padilla would otherwise enjoy as a U.S. citizen. Refusing to deal with either argument, Chief Justice William Rehnquist's 5–4 majority opinion ruled that Padilla had filed his petition for review of the grounds of his detention in the wrong federal district and would have to refile in the federal district in which he was detained. Writing for the dissenters, Justice John Paul Stevens would have held that the Southern District had jurisdiction and that Padilla was entitled to a review of his detention there.

In *Hamdi v. Rumsfeld* (124 S. Ct. 2633 [2004]), the Court did reach the merits. Yaser Esam Hamdi was seized by Coalition forces on the battlefield in Afghanistan in fall 2001. He was brought to the U.S. naval base at Guantanamo Bay, Cuba, for detention as an enemy combatant, but when the army discovered that Hamdi was a U.S. citizen (he was born in Louisiana, but grew up in Saudi Arabia), he was transferred to a military brig in Virginia and was later moved to one in South Carolina. At the time the Court heard his case, Hamdi had been held for more than two years inside the United States without charge, trial, or access to counsel. Hamdi's lawyers argued that as a U.S. citizen, he was entitled to the full panoply of protections afforded by the Constitution to those accused of criminal offenses. Justice Sandra Day O'Connor wrote for a bare plurality, including Chief Justice Rehnquist, Justice Anthony Kennedy, and Justice Stephen Breyer. She held that Congress had formally authorized the use of military force against al Qaeda and the Taliban, and that under that authorization, the government, as it contended, could detain as an enemy combatant even a U.S. citizen on U.S. soil who had joined the wartime adversary of the United States. But such a designation, she also ruled, did not altogether nullify citizen Hamdi's constitutional protections: Hamdi had the right to challenge, with the aid of a lawyer and before a neutral decision maker, his designation as an enemy combatant. Justice David Souter's concurring opinion, joined by Justice Ruth Bader Ginsburg, denied that Hamdi's detention had been properly authorized by Congress but affirmed the plurality position that Hamdi was entitled to a meaningful review of the government's reasons for detaining him.

In a strange pairing, Justice Antonin Scalia, joined by Justice Stevens, drew a bright line, arguing in dissent that the government lacked constitutional authority to hold a U.S. citizen in the United States as an enemy combatant. The Constitution, in Scalia's view, gave the government only two options: It could charge Hamdi with treason, or Congress could suspend the writ of habeas corpus. Justice Clarence Thomas, in dissent, rejected the propriety of the Court's intervention. He argued that although the plurality had properly concluded that the congressional authorization of the use of military force provided the president with the power to designate citizens as enemy combatants, courts nevertheless lacked the information and the expertise to determine whether Hamdi was accurately so designated; therefore, the Court was obligated to leave the matter to the discretion granted to the president in wartime by the Constitution.

In *Rasul v. Bush* (124 S. Ct. 2686 [2004]), a 6–3 majority of the Court went further, revealing still sharper divisions among the justices. Circumventing a half-century-old precedent, it ruled that *alien* enemy combatants captured in Afghanistan and held at the U.S. naval base at Guantanamo Bay were entitled to challenge their detentions in U.S. federal court. Justice Stevens's majority opinion emphasized that although the United States did not exercise "ultimate sovereignty" over Guantanamo Bay, which still belonged to Cuba, the long-term leasing arrangement into which the United States had entered in 1903 brought the territory where the Guantanamo detainees were held under the "plenary and exclusive jurisdiction" of the

United States. Yet Stevens also used language that suggested a more sweeping holding—that alien enemy combatants held by U.S. forces *anywhere* in the world could seek relief in U.S. federal courts. In an angry dissent, joined by Chief Justice Rehnquist and Justice Thomas, Justice Scalia declared that the Court produced a ruling that not only had no foundation in the Constitution or previous law but also that would impose an immense burden on the U.S. military, requiring it to divert time, energy, and resources from battlefields around the world to judicial proceedings in U.S. federal courts.

The enemy combatant cases represent the leading edge of U.S. efforts to devise legal rules, consistent with American constitutional principles and the laws of war, for waging the global war on terror. As the distinguished contributors to this volume demonstrate, *Padilla*, *Hamdi*, and *Rasul* raise crucial questions about the balance between national security and civil liberties in wartime; they generate knotty separation of powers issues; and they call upon the courts, the political branches, and the country to reexamine the complicated connections between the Constitution and international law. Spanning the spectrum of informed legal opinion, the essays gathered here show that debating the enemy combatant cases is indispensable to meeting the legal challenges to come in the long war that lies ahead.

Seth Waxman puts the cases in historical and theoretical perspective. His point of departure is the confidence that Justice O'Connor expresses in *Hamdi* that today's courts will prove up to the task of balancing civil liberties and national security. Although he applauds O'Connor's decision and hopes time will vindicate her confidence, Waxman observes that the Court's conduct during past national security crises scarcely justifies optimism. In late eighteenth-century hostilities with France, during the Civil War, and in World War II, the Court showed a pronounced deference to the executive branch's penchant for overriding the claims of liberty in the name of security. So why has the current Court displayed considerably less deference to the executive branch and provided, in the enemy combatant cases, significantly more protection for civil liberties? Waxman offers two paradigms for explaining the departure. One views the enemy combatant cases from the perspective of "crisis jurisprudence" and suggests a variety of explanations: Over time, the Court has learned from its mistakes; civil liberties precedents have achieved a critical mass; as war comes to be seen as a constant feature of the political landscape, judges cannot postpone the preservation of individual liberty to peacetime; and as the immediate threat of September 11 recedes, the Supreme Court has grown less inclined to show deference to national security interests. The other paradigm focuses on changes in the Court's perception of its institutional powers. From this perspective, the Court's enemy combatant decisions may reflect its steadily increasing confidence and assertiveness over the past several decades. Although it is too early to identify accurately the balance of factors involved, in all likelihood, both paradigms are needed to account for the Court's reluctance in the present war to defer to executive branch judgment.

Judge Patricia Wald focuses on the doctrinal puzzles to which the enemy combatant cases give rise. But first she insists that the Court was right to hear the cases. The question of the Court's job in war, she points out, is part of a larger and long-standing political and academic debate about "the appropriate role of the judiciary in the complex social, economic, and moral issues of our national life." Given the civil liberties questions at stake, she applauds the Court's entry into the controversy. Yet she also believes the Court's hand was forced. Had the enemy combatant cases involved the possibility of a solution along federalism lines using the fifty states as laboratories, or had Congress attempted legislative action or even held hearings to explore what should be done with al Qaeda members after they had been captured, or had the executive branch shown greater respect for the process owed detainees under international law, she believes the Court might not have felt compelled to intervene as forcefully as it did. Although Wald largely agrees with the Court's judgments, she concentrates on elaborating a variety of big questions that remain unanswered by the enemy combatant cases: Does habeas lie for foreign detainees housed elsewhere than at Guantanamo? Does it lie for claims of abuse or violations of international law apart from total innocence of being a combatant at all? Do foreigners have the same rights at a habeas hearing as do American-born defendants? How far can the designation of "enemy combatant" carry beyond the battlefield? Do targets of intelligence covert actions abroad have any rights comparable with enemy combatants? She concludes that these critical questions are not of the kind that the Court can resolve alone. Rather, they demand responses that are, in significant measure, legislative in nature, and so require Congress to accept its responsibility in waging the global war on terror.

Like Judge Wald, John Yoo thinks that the Court alone cannot provide all the solutions to questions posed by the enemy combatant cases. But Yoo believes that the Court did more to limit its involvement than is commonly perceived. According to the conventional wisdom, the cases "dealt the Bush administration a defeat in the war on terrorism." The reality, Yoo argues, is more complicated. In fact, the Court embraced the administration's "fundamental legal approach" by agreeing that the country was at war with a new kind of enemy, that Congress had authorized that war, and that U.S. citizens fighting on al Qaeda's side could be detained as enemy combatants. Yet Yoo also contends that with its rulings in *Hamdi* and *Rasul*, the Court "took a wrong turn and overstepped the traditional boundaries of judicial review." The Court thereby unwisely injected itself into military matters and "thrust the federal courts into the center of policy making in the war on terrorism." The crux of the problem is that compared with the political branches, courts lack competence in foreign policy and national security. Their comparative disadvantage in these areas, Yoo argues, stems both from the nature of the adversarial process and the structure of the federal judiciary. American federal courts present high barriers to access, they impose severe limits on the acquisition and processing of information, their role is limited to the interpretation of the law, and they are poorly situated to adjudicate issues involving the ambiguities of international law. At the same time, the federal judiciary tends to select for generalists who lack the specialized knowledge that national security and foreign policy questions require; with its ninety-two district courts and thirteen courts of appeals, the federal judiciary is highly decentralized and, therefore, could create a multiplicity of opinions in a domain where the Constitution aims to centralize functions and project a single voice; and the federal judiciary proceeds very slowly, whereas national security and foreign policy questions often require rapid responses. Accordingly, in Yoo's view, the Court ought to refrain from entangling itself any further in the review of the military's handling of enemy combatants and leave the matter to the political branches.

Benjamin Wittes explores the variety of institutions and actors that shaped the outcome in the enemy combatant cases. Although he agrees with the conventional wisdom that the cases represent a "stinging rebuke" to the Bush administration, Wittes also agrees with John Yoo that the Court endorsed the administration's "fundamental approach." And though he admires the manner in which the Court balanced constitutional values in *Hamdi*, he is also in agreement with Yoo that it went too far in *Rasul*, sidestepping the governing precedent in an utterly unconvincing manner. But Wittes believes that the Court is far from alone in having failed to rise to the occasion. He does not quarrel with the administration's "desire to use the traditional presidential wartime powers to detain enemy combatants," but he does criticize it for its "Article II fundamentalism"—for acting, that is, as if decisions about enemy combatants were purely a matter of executive discretion and not also legislative in nature. Congress made matters worse by failing to assert its responsibility to legislate in the face of the challenges presented by al Qaeda. Wittes also faults human rights and civil liberties groups. They played a major role by filing amicus briefs in the cases and presenting the Court with a prominent alternative to the administration's Article II fundamentalism. Unfortunately, Wittes observes, the alternative put forward by these groups embodied an extreme civil liberties fundamentalism that was both unpragmatic and tendentious in its reading of settled doctrine. In the face of this array of failures, Wittes expresses sympathy for the Court's "desire to split the baby between the claims of liberty and the claims of military necessity." But, echoing Judge Wald, Wittes would much prefer "a serious and deliberative legislative process," which would require not only a more engaged and responsible Congress but also an executive branch more attuned to the limits of its powers and a human rights and civil liberties community more appreciative of wartime exigencies and the laws of war.

Mark Tushnet is less sanguine that the Court can be kept in check. This is because of the "perfect Constitution" assumption, which he argues is pervasive in constitutional theory and Supreme Court jurisprudence and indeed "nearly inescapable." According to this assumption, the Constitution, properly construed, "is entirely adequate to meet the perceived needs of contemporary society." This assumption, argues Tushnet, is at work in all the opinions in *Hamdi*. In her plurality opinion, Justice O'Connor concludes both that the Constitution provides the president with all the power he needs to detain an alleged enemy combatant and that the Constitution prescribes a method for determining the process constitutionally due such a detainee. Justice Souter's concurrence adopts the assumption by suggesting that though the president cannot detain a U.S. citizen without express congressional authorization, the Constitution may permit executive detention in times of "genuine emergency." Justice Scalia's sharp dissent draws upon the assumption in arguing that the Constitution gave to the president a perfectly clear choice in responding to a captured citizen enemy combatant: Prosecute for treason or suspend habeas corpus. And Justice Thomas's dissent relied upon it by declaring, "[T]he Federal government has all power necessary to protect the Nation." Of course, the Court can limit the reach of the perfect Constitution assumption by declaring questions nonjusticiable or properly left for resolution by the political branches. But the justices are inclined to proceed from the assumption, Tushnet argues, because they feel a responsibility to provide solutions to the nation's urgent problems and because, under the cover of the assumption, they can place responsibility for controversial outcomes on those who long ago wrote and ratified the Constitution. However, the cost of the assumption is, in Tushnet's eyes, considerable. Most significantly, it leads the Court to twist constitutional text and its own precedents while depriving the political branches and the public of the opportunity to have their say on weighty questions of national interest.

Ruth Wedgwood brings the volume to a close by examining the questions that the Guantanamo controversy raises about the limits of law, and particularly about the judicial adjudication of legal disputes, in wartime. *Rasul* placed the Court in unfamiliar territory because "the capture and internment of prisoners of war and irregular combatants in overseas military operations has not generally engaged the attention of civilian judges." And the Court did not acquit itself well, in Wedgwood's view. In deciding that enemy combatants held at Guantanamo Bay could challenge their detention in federal court, the Court proceeded with too little regard for precedent, too little attention to the canons of statutory construction, too little thought to whether federal law provided any substantive relief for alien enemy combatants, and too little concern for the implications of its holding for the waging of war. Wedgwood notes that in subsequent litigation, enemy combatants might search for substantive law in a variety of sources: the U.S. Constitution, treaties, customary international law (also called "the laws and customs of war" or "international humanitarian law"), and statutes. But all, she shows, pose significant problems. Accordingly, "federal courts will, at a minimum, need to be aware of their limitations in seeking to draw upon these intricate sources of law, especially in the minefield of military operations."

Despite her serious criticisms of *Rasul*, Wedgwood appreciates the Court's reasons for taking action: the desire of the justices to weigh in on the momentuous legal questions raised by the government's actions taken after September 11; the abuses at Abu Ghraib; and the Office of Legal Council memos, which suggested an almost boundless executive power in the conduct of war. Indeed, she speculates that the Court "may be inclined to maintain a type of 'strategic ambiguity' on questions of review, in order to summon the executive branch and Congress to appropriate moral attention." In the end, though, she believes it should primarily be left to the political branches, by virtue of their superior tools and broader knowledge, to take the lead in crafting a new legal regime for the handling of enemy combatants and such other challenges as are bound to arise in the global war on terror.

The debate that the contributors to this volume have joined is still in its early stages, but thanks to their analysis and arguments, the key issues have come into better focus. Although they differ in their judgments about the proper extent of the Court's involvement in the enemy combatant cases, the other contributors are in agreement with Judge Wald that with the September 11 attacks, the United States found itself engaged "in a new kind of war, with new dilemmas that needed new rules." If they disagree as to the details of the new legal regime that the country is in the process of crafting, all are in agreement that each of the three branches of government must rise to the occasion and that each must perform its constitutional share of the labors, which includes defending against encroachment by other branches. Finally, the contributors are emphatic in agreement that fortifying the rule of law at home is itself both a demand of justice and a national security imperative.

1. The Combatant Detention Trilogy Through the Lenses of History

Seth P. Waxman

HIDDEN WITHIN Justice Sandra Day O'Connor's opinion in *Hamdi v. Rumsfeld* is a remarkable sentence that has gone largely unnoticed in early commentaries on the decision. Concluding her discussion of the process a lower court might require when considering a habeas corpus petition from an alleged enemy combatant, Justice O'Connor wrote:

> We have no reason to doubt that courts faced with these sensitive matters will pay proper heed both to the matters of national security that might arise in an individual case and to the constitutional limitations safeguarding essential liberties that remain vibrant even in times of security concerns.[1]

Although this passage is not essential to the Court's holding or reasoning, it is nonetheless important and surprising. Prior to the announcement of the combatant detention decisions, few judges, lawyers, or scholars would necessarily have shared Justice O'Connor's expression of confidence in the courts' ability to balance liberty and security in moments of crisis. In fact, before *Hamdi*, *Padilla*, and

---

1. *Hamdi v. Rumsfeld*, 124 S. Ct. 2633, 2652 (2004).

Rasul, conventional wisdom was that the courts, including the Supreme Court, were poor guardians of liberty during periods of perceived threats to national security.

Yet Justice O'Connor seemed wholly unsurprised that the Court could maintain the difficult and delicate equilibrium between national security and individual liberty. If her confidence was justified—as I hope time will show it was—why did the Court act differently in these cases than it has during previous national security crises? In this essay, I explore two paradigms for answering that question.

The first paradigm places the combatant detention decisions in the context of earlier cases involving individual liberties during war. Several judges and scholars have suggested that the Supreme Court's behavior in these episodes has followed a disappointing cycle of giving excessive weight to national security concerns while a military conflict is active, correcting only partially and regretfully for the damage to individual liberties once security has been restored. The combatant detention cases—coming fewer than three years after September 11, with U.S. troops still fighting two wars overseas, yet striking a strong note of restraint on executive power—seem to break this cycle. But if they do, where does the explanation lie? In the unusual nature of the war in which the nation is engaged? In the executive branch's political and legal overreaching? In the Court's having learned from its earlier mistakes? Or perhaps the very premise of the question is wrong, and there has been no cycle from which the recent cases diverge.

A second lens through which to view these cases is that of interbranch relations and the institutional confidence of the Supreme Court. On this view, the most illuminating points of comparison are not earlier wartime decisions, but rather the nonnational security cases that illustrate the Court's growing self-confidence since World War II in its relations with the other branches of the national government. Perhaps the Court's affirmation of individual rights in the combatant detention cases is a product of this broader rise in judicial assertiveness. The current Court has often accomplished this expansion of its power through a strategy of "judicial minimalism," the practice of circumscribing the specific holdings of individual cases.[2] The detainee cases can be seen as products of a powerful, though restrained, Court.

I.

The view that the Court's wartime jurisprudence reflects a cycle of excessive deference to the executive branch's national security concerns followed by belated affirmations of individual rights has been shared by observers across the political spectrum. For example, Justice William Brennan and Chief Justice William Rehnquist—an unlikely pair of intellectual bedfellows—have been two of the most thoughtful proponents of this cycle thesis. In a 1987 lecture at Hebrew University in Jerusalem, Justice Brennan said:

> The trouble in the United States . . . has been not so much the refusal to recognize principles of civil liberties during times of war and national crisis but rather the reluctance and inability to question, during the period of panic, asserted wartime dangers with which the nation and the judiciary [are] unfamiliar. . . . After each perceived security crisis ended, the United States has remorsefully realized that the abrogation of civil liberties was unnecessary. But it has proven unable to prevent itself from repeating the error when the next crisis came along.[3]

Chief Justice Rehnquist echoed the same theme in his intriguing book, *All the Laws but One: Civil Liberties in Wartime*. When discussing the application of Cicero's famous adage, *inter arma silent*

---

2. CASS SUNSTEIN, ONE CASE AT A TIME: JUDICIAL MINIMALISM ON THE SUPREME COURT (1999).

3. Willam J. Brennan, Jr., *The Quest to Develop a Jurisprudence of Civil Liberties in Times of Security Crises*, ISR. YEARBOOK ON HUMAN RIGHTS, 11, 16–17 (1988).

leges, "during war law is silent," to the American experience, the Chief Justice wrote:

> [T]he maxim speaks to the timing of a judicial decision on a question of civil liberty in wartime. If the decision is made after hostilities have ceased, it is more likely to favor civil liberty than if made while hostilities continue. The contrast between the *Quirin* and the Japanese internment decisions on the one hand and the *Milligan* and *Duncan* decisions on the other show[s] that this, too, is a historically accurate observation about the American system. . . . There is no reason to think that future wartime presidents will act differently from Lincoln, Wilson, or Roosevelt, or that future Justices of the Supreme Court will decide questions differently from their predecessors.[4]

Both Brennan and Rehnquist cogently described a recurring cycle in American history: a government crackdown on civil liberties during the crisis that is sustained by the courts, followed by a judicial reconsideration once the crisis has passed, and then forgetfulness when the next crisis emerges.

This cyclical pattern first appeared in the early days of the Republic. In 1798, only fifteen years after the end of the Revolutionary War and less than a decade after ratification of the Constitution, the young United States found itself embroiled in an international crisis. With war between the United States and France looming, the Federalist-dominated Congress passed a series of laws that severely restricted individual rights, especially those of the political opposition. The Sedition Act, in particular, made it a federal crime to "write, print, utter or publish . . . any false, scandalous and malicious writing or writings against the government of the United States, or the President of the United States, with the intent to defame . . . or to bring them . . . into contempt or disrepute."[5]

---

4. WILLIAM H. REHNQUIST, ALL THE LAWS BUT ONE: CIVIL LIBERTIES IN WARTIME 224 (1998).
    5. Act of July 14, 1798, ch. 74, § 2, 1 Stat. 596. The companion Alien Act and

These acts quickly became weapons to silence Thomas Jefferson's emerging pro-French Republican Party. The government initiated more than two dozen prosecutions under the Sedition Act—all against members of the political opposition, including four leading Republican newspaper editors and three Republican officeholders. In the most famous case, Congressman Matthew Lyon spent four months in prison for publishing materials criticizing President John Adams.[6]

Consistent with the pattern Justice Brennan and Chief Justice Rehnquist have described, the courts refused to protect freedom of expression during this early crisis period. Although the Supreme Court never ruled on the Sedition Act, several lower-court judges, including three Supreme Court justices sitting on circuit, upheld the law.[7] The Federalist-dominated judiciary sometimes even aided the prosecution. During Lyon's trial, for example, the judge told the jury that it only had to decide two issues: whether Lyon had published the pieces and whether the pieces were seditious. In one representative case, the judge instructed the jury that "[i]f a man attempts to destroy the confidence of the people in their officers, their supreme magistrate, and their legislature, he effectually saps the foundation of the government."[8]

Once the quasi war with France cooled off, public hostility to the acts helped to defeat the Federalists and bring Jefferson and his party to power in the elections of 1800. Jefferson quickly pardoned those who had been convicted under the acts, and the new Congress refused to renew the acts when they were reconsidered in 1801.

---

the Alien Enemies Act gave the president the power to deport aliens suspected of activities posing a threat to the national government and to imprison all subjects of warring foreign nations as enemy aliens (Act of July 6, 1798, ch. 58, 1 Stat. 571).

6. *See* MICHAEL KENT CURTIS, FREE SPEECH, "THE PEOPLE'S DARLING PRIVILEGE:" STRUGGLES FOR FREEDOM OF EXPRESSION IN AMERICAN HISTORY 80–85 (2000).

7. GEOFFREY R. STONE ET AL., THE FIRST AMENDMENT 8 (1999).

8. CURTIS, at 90.

Although these laws were quickly denounced as working outrageous deprivations of liberty, the courts did not officially redeem themselves until 1964, when, in *New York Times Co. v. Sullivan*, the Supreme Court concluded that "[a]lthough the Sedition Act was never tested in the Court, the attack upon its validity has carried the day in the court of history"[9] (footnote omitted).

The court of history took a long time to render its verdict, though, because during America's next major national security crisis, the Civil War, the government again took several actions that threatened basic constitutional rights in the name of national security. Over the course of the war, President Abraham Lincoln's suspension of the writ of habeas corpus and imposition of martial law led to the arrest of more than 13,000 civilians. At first, these presidential orders were restricted to areas near lines of combat, but they were soon expanded to encompass the entire country.[10]

Apart from the slight wrinkle of *Ex parte Merryman*, which I address later, the Supreme Court did not have an opportunity to review these measures until after Robert E. Lee had surrendered at Appomattox. In *Ex parte Milligan*, decided more than a year after the war had ended, the Court finally condemned the deprivations that took place during the war. All nine justices agreed that President Lincoln lacked the constitutional authority to suspend the writ and establish a system of military justice in areas where civilian courts were open and operating. In sweeping language, the Court said, "Martial law . . . destroys every guarantee of the Constitution. . . . Civil liberty and this kind of martial law cannot endure together; the antagonism is irreconcilable; and, in the conflict, one or the other must perish."[11] At the same time, however, the Court acknowledged its own institutional limitations in times of crisis. Almost sheepishly, the *Milligan* Court confessed:

9. *New York Times Co. v. Sullivan*, 376 U.S. 254, 276 (1964).
10. DANIEL FARBER, LINCOLN'S CONSTITUTION 157–63 (2003).
11. *Ex parte Milligan*, 71 U.S. 2, 124–25 (1866).

During the late wicked Rebellion, the temper of the times did not allow that calmness in deliberation and discussion so necessary to a correct conclusion of a purely judicial question. *Then*, considerations of safety were mingled with the exercise of power; and feelings and interests prevailed which are happily terminated. *Now* that the public safety is assured, this question, as well as all others, can be discussed and decided without passion or the admixture of any element not required to form a legal judgment.[12]

With its self-conscious recognition that the Court was only able to offer those protections because peace and a sense of security had been reestablished, *Milligan* stands as a symbol of both judicial strength and judicial weakness in the face of executive national security claims.

The Brennan/Rehnquist cycle repeated itself during World War I. Shortly after the United States entered the war, President Woodrow Wilson persuaded Congress to enact the Espionage Act of 1917. The act made it a crime to make "false statements with the intent to interfere with the operation or success of the military or naval forces of the United States" or "to cause insubordination, disloyalty, mutiny or refusal of duty" in the military or interfere with military recruitment.[13] One year later, Congress bolstered the government's powers by passing the Sedition Act, which made it illegal to willfully "utter, print, write, or publish any disloyal, profane, scurrilous, or abusive language about" the U.S. form of government; its Constitution, flag, military forces, or uniform; "or any language intended to bring the [same] into contempt . . . or disrepute."[14]

More than 2,000 individuals were prosecuted under these laws. Many of the victims were socialists who had simply denounced the war as a capitalist plot. In several cases, the only evidence used to

---

12. *Id.* at 109.
13. Espionage Act of 1917, ch. 30, § 3, 40 Stat. 217, 219.
14. Sedition Act of 1918, ch. 75, § 3, 40 Stat. 553.

demonstrate the falsity of the defendant's statements were speeches to the contrary by President Wilson or Congress's resolution supporting the war.[15]

The Supreme Court upheld the constitutionality of the Espionage Act in three terse opinions issued on the same day in 1919. Those decisions were announced a year after World War I had ended but in the midst of another crisis, the first "Red Scare," orchestrated in response to the Russian Revolution. In the leading case, *Schenck v. United States*, Justice Oliver Wendell Holmes wrote:

> The question in every case is whether the words used are used in such circumstances and are of such a nature as to create a *clear and present danger* that they will bring about the substantive evils that Congress has a right to prevent. . . . When a nation is at war many things that might be said in times of peace are such a hindrance to its effort that their utterance will not be endured so long as men fight and that no Court could regard them as protected by any constitutional right.[16] (emphasis added)

When the Court applied this clear-and-present-danger test to both the Espionage and Sedition Acts, it affirmed the convictions of defendants like Charles Schenck, Eugene V. Debs, and Jacob Abrams—men who did nothing more than distribute pamphlets criticizing the draft, write in opposition to the war, or, at worst, urge those drafted to disobey the selective service order.[17]

In 1969, the Supreme Court finally corrected for this rights-restrictive application of the clear-and-present-danger test. In *Brandenburg v. Ohio*, the Court held that the government may not prohibit "advocacy of the use of force or of law violation except where such advocacy is directed to inciting or producing imminent lawless

---

15. Brennan, at 15.

16. *Schenck v. United States*, 249 U.S. 47, 52 (1919).

17. *Id.*; *Debs v. United States*, 249 U.S. 211 (1919); *Abrams v. United States*, 250 U.S. 616 (1919).

action and is likely to incite or produce such action."[18] This more protective test has survived until today as a robust guarantor of the right to free expression. Coming so long after the World War I panic had ended, though, the *Brandenburg* test also demonstrates how the crisis cycle again held true: The Court needed the wisdom of hindsight and the cloak of peacetime to enable it to strongly defend basic civil liberties.

My final example, *Korematsu v. United States*, is the case most commonly associated with the cycle. The history of the Japanese internment and the Supreme Court's tragic response is so well known that a brief description will suffice. During the Second World War, President Franklin Roosevelt signed Executive Order 9066, authorizing curfews and the removal of all people of Japanese descent from the Pacific coast. Under this order, more than 120,000 people were transported to "relocation centers," where some remained for up to four years.[19] Japanese internment was, as Eugene Rostow wrote in 1945, "the worst blow our liberties ha[d] sustained in many years."[20]

As war raged, the Supreme Court found the curfews and exclusion of citizens of Japanese ancestry to be constitutional. Upholding the president's executive order, Justice Hugo Black wrote that the court was "unable to conclude that it was beyond the war power of Congress and the Executive to exclude those of Japanese ancestry from the West Coast war area at the time they did." He further stated:

> [W]e are not unmindful of the hardships imposed by it upon a large group of American citizens. But hardships are part of war, and war is an aggregation of hardships. All citizens alike, both in and out of uniform, feel the impact of war in greater or lesser

18. *Brandenburg v. Ohio*, 395 U.S. 444, 447 (1969).

19. Philip Tajitsu Nash, *Moving for Redress*, 94 YALE L.J. 743, 743 (1985) (reviewing JOHN TATEISHI, AND JUSTICE FOR ALL: AN ORAL HISTORY OF THE JAPANESE AMERICAN DETENTION CAMPS [1984]).

20. Eugene V. Rostow, *The Japanese American Cases—A Disaster*, 54 YALE L.J. 489, 490 (1945).

measure. Citizenship has its responsibilities as well as its privileges, and in time of war the burden is always heavier.[21]

Even the order's base racial distinctions were not enough to overcome the pressure to support repressive wartime policies justified on national security grounds. To this day, *Korematsu* stands as the Court's greatest failure to protect civil liberties during a crisis.

Once the crisis had ended, the judiciary retrospectively corrected in part for the excesses of *Korematsu*. In 1946, the Supreme Court considered a case arising out of the wartime imposition of martial law in Hawaii. Following Japan's surrender, and more than a year after martial law had been terminated, the Court heard an appeal in *Duncan v. Kahanamoku*, arising from a civilian's court-martial conviction for assaulting U.S. Marine officers. Citing *Milligan*, Justice Black, the author of *Korematsu*, found that the imposition of martial law had been unlawful. "Our system of government," the Court now felt comfortable to say, "clearly is the antithesis of total military rule and the founders of this country are not likely to have contemplated complete military dominance within the limits of a territory made part of this country and not recently taken from an enemy."[22] In effect, the Court reaffirmed the important principle that the judiciary must protect citizens' constitutional rights and protect the separation of powers, even under conditions of war. It only did so, however, after the war had ended.[23]

---

21. *Korematsu v. United States*, 323 U.S. 214, 217, 219 (1944).

22. *Duncan v. Kahanamoku*, 327 U.S. 304, 322 (1946).

23. More symbolically, in 1984, a district court granted a rare writ of *coram nobis* and vacated Fred Korematsu's conviction. Relying on the report of a congressional commission formed to study the Japanese internment and provide remedies for its victims, the court found that the government had supplied the Supreme Court with incorrect facts about the Japanese-American threat. It then concluded with words that are characteristic of the curative, cathartic portion of the cycle:

> *Korematsu* remains on the pages of our legal and political history. As a legal precedent it is now recognized as having very limited application. As historical precedent it stands as a constant caution that in times of war or declared military necessity our institutions must be vigilant in

And then came September 11, which one might have expected to trigger another iteration of this historical cycle. When the Supreme Court heard arguments in the three combatant detention cases, the United States was still embedded in a national security crisis. Almost daily, the front pages warned of impending al Qaeda attacks on American targets. In fact, on April 20, 2004—the day the Guantanamo cases were argued—the *Washington Post* published an article entitled: "Precautions Raised for Preelection Terrorism; Al Qaeda Intends to Strike, Officials Say."[24] The Department of Homeland Security's threat advisory levels consistently stood at yellow or orange. American troops were still actively engaged in both Afghanistan and Iraq. Only days before the government submitted its brief in the *Padilla* case, al Qaeda affiliates launched their devastating March 11 attacks in Madrid. Osama bin Laden and several of his deputies remained at large and continued to issue threats against the United States and its allies. What President George W. Bush told the country on September 20, 2001—"Americans should not expect one battle, but a lengthy campaign"—had not changed almost three years after the opening salvos of the war on terror.[25] In short, the crisis was active, dangerous, and ongoing.

If the patterns of the past were to be repeated, one might have expected a set of Supreme Court opinions that undervalued civil lib-

---

protecting constitutional guarantees. It stands as a caution that in times of distress the shield of military necessity and national security must not be used to protect governmental actions from close scrutiny and accountability. It stands as a caution that in times of international hostility and antagonisms our institutions, legislative, executive and judicial, must be prepared to exercise their authority to protect all citizens from the petty fears and prejudices that are so easily aroused."

Korematsu v. United States, 584 F. Supp. 1406, 1420 (N.D. Cal. 1984).

24. John Mintz, *Precautions Raised for Preelection Terrorism; Al Qaeda Intends to Strike, Officials Say*, WASH. POST, Apr. 20, 2004, at A3.

25. George W. Bush, address to a Joint Session of Congress and the American People (Sept. 20, 2001), available at http://www.whitehouse.gov/news/releases/2001/09/20010920-8.html.

erties in a classic wartime tradeoff with national security. The Brennan/Rehnquist cycle would have predicted decisions that upheld the constitutionality of the indefinite detention of American citizens as "enemy combatants." If the cycle had unfolded as it had in the examples discussed earlier, the Court would have agreed with the government that the Commander-in-Chief Clause or Congress's Authorization for the Use of Military Force (AUMF) in Afghanistan broadly empowered the president to hold Jose Padilla and Yaser Hamdi without charge, trial, or access to counsel. An opinion consistent with the cycle would have held that Article III courts lacked jurisdiction to hear habeas cases brought by those held at Guantanamo Bay or by any other noncitizen detained outside the territorial jurisdiction of the United States. We would have had to wait until the crisis passed for corrective decisions.

Both the rhetoric and the substance of the combatant detention decisions, however, were far more protective of civil liberties than continuation of the cycle would have foretold. One cannot readily imagine past Courts following through on Justice O'Connor's declaration in *Hamdi* that "a state of war is not a blank check for the President when it comes to the rights of the Nation's citizens."[26] On the surface, at least, these cases do not fit neatly into the cyclical historical pattern. The decisions do not give in to the executive branch's views about the demands of national security (or offer repentant post hoc protection for civil liberties). Instead, in what the Court understood to be the midst of a "war," the decisions explicitly account for the substantial competing interests that lie on both sides of the constitutional scale.

In *Hamdi*, the plurality first offered a circumscribed holding on the threshold question of whether the executive has the authority to detain citizens as "enemy combatants." Justice O'Connor and the three justices who joined her found that the congressional resolution

26. *Hamdi*, 124 S. Ct. at 2650 (2004).

authorizing military force did, in fact, permit such detentions. The plurality was careful, however, to limit the scope of that authorization to citizens who are "'part of or supporting forces hostile to the United States or coalition partners' *in Afghanistan* and who 'engaged in an armed conflict against the United States' there"[27] (emphasis added).

Unlike in past cases decided in the midst of a war, both sides could find favorable aspects of this holding. On the one hand, the executive could take comfort in the fact that the Court held not only that the AUMF authorized the detention of certain U.S.-citizen enemy combatants, but also that it satisfied 18 U.S.C. § 4001, a previously little-known statute that provides that "[n]o citizen shall be imprisoned or otherwise detained by the United States except pursuant to an Act of Congress." Attorneys for both Hamdi and Padilla had forcefully argued that Section 4001 barred the detention of their clients because the AUMF lacked a clear congressional statement authorizing their imprisonment. Justice O'Connor's opinion rejected this position:

> It is of no moment that the AUMF does not use specific language of detention. Because detention to prevent a combatant's return to the battlefield is a fundamental incident of waging war, in permitting the use of "necessary and appropriate force," Congress has clearly and unmistakably authorized detention in the narrow circumstances considered here.[28]

So, however narrow the category may be, the Court did find a category of individuals who could be detained as enemy combatants. Finally, the Court also accepted the government's argument that citizenship did not bar detention as an enemy combatant.

At the same time, *Hamdi* was more protective of civil liberties than past cases decided during a national security threat had been. For example, in addition to limiting its holding to active, enemy

27. *Id.* at 2639.
28. *Id.* at 2641.

soldiers captured in Afghanistan, the Court avoided the question of
whether the president's Article II commander-in-chief powers provided him with the authority to detain Hamdi. When given an opportunity to issue a broad endorsement of executive power in this crisis,
the Supreme Court abstained. Moreover, the Court demonstrated a
special concern for the prospect of indefinite detention. It specifically
rejected one of the government's leading justifications for the continued detention of Yaser Hamdi and other enemy combatants: an ongoing need to extract intelligence information from captured al Qaeda
members. The Court stated that "indefinite detention for the purpose
of interrogation is not authorized" by the AUMF.[29] Instead, the Court
again limited its holding to the facts of the case, finding that detention
is authorized only as long as active combat operations continue in
Afghanistan.

One of the more provocative aspects of Justice O'Connor's plurality opinion is its explication of the process that is constitutionally
owed to a detained enemy combatant. Here, the very methodology
applied by the Court signals a profound departure from past midcrisis
decisions. The Court turned to the handy *Mathews v. Eldridge* cal-
culus, under which a court explicitly balances the private interests
that will be affected by a proposed process with the government's own
interests, including the cost to the government for providing a greater
process. By employing this test, the Court imposed upon itself a
framework that would take into account both the liberty and the security interests at stake in the case.

More important, the plurality's opinion thoughtfully carries out
this balancing. The Court held that a citizen detainee was entitled,
at minimum, to notice of the factual basis for his classification as an
enemy combatant, an opportunity to rebut that classification before
a neutral decision maker, and, probably, access to counsel during
these proceedings. Refusing to accept the executive's appeal to overriding security concerns, the plurality wrote:

29. *Id.*

> Nor is the weight on this side of the *Mathews* scale offset by the circumstances of war. . . . [A]s critical as the Government's interest may be in detaining those who actually pose an immediate threat to the national security of the United States during ongoing international conflict, history and common sense teach us that an unchecked system of detention carries the potential to become a means for oppression and abuse of others who do not present that sort of threat.[30]

In fact, this passage conspicuously cites *Milligan*—a case from the later, corrective phase of an earlier cycle—for support.

However, the plurality opinion does not completely ignore the important national security side of the balance. It explicitly recognized that "aside from these core elements, enemy-combatant proceedings may be tailored to alleviate their uncommon potential to burden the Executive at a time of ongoing military conflict."[31] In the end, while the Court found the government's proposed "some evidence" standard to be inadequate, it also allowed for a presumption in favor of the government, the admission of hearsay evidence, or even the use of military tribunals to decide the fate of alleged enemy combatants.[32] As I discuss below, the exact practical effects of this balancing remains to be seen. But the product of the *Hamdi* balancing is a set of minimum constitutional requirements that differ strikingly from those that appeared in past examples of the Brennan/Rehnquist cycle.

Likewise, in determining that the Guantanamo Bay detainees could petition for habeas corpus in federal courts, *Rasul v. Bush* was also more protective of civil liberties than the cycle might have predicted. Even Justice Anthony Kennedy's concurrence, which applied *Johnson v. Eisentrager* to find jurisdiction over the detainees based on America's de facto sovereignty over Guantanamo Bay, represented a

30. *Id.* at 2647.
31. *Id.* at 2649.
32. *Id.*

considerable departure from the Court's earlier wartime rulings. That
Justice John Paul Stevens's opinion for the Court went beyond Justice
Kennedy's proposed constitutional holding was especially surprising.

The majority found jurisdiction on the basis of the habeas statute, finding that the statute did not distinguish between Americans
and aliens held in federal custody. In particular, the Court stated that
"there is little reason to think that Congress intended the geographical
coverage of the statute to vary depending on the detainee's citizenship."[33] Because the government conceded that the courts would
have jurisdiction over *citizens* held at Guantanamo Bay, the majority
concluded that the habeas statute must also confer jurisdiction over
aliens held there.[34] The Court also drew support from the historical
reach of common-law habeas corpus, which traditionally had
extended beyond the sovereign territory of the crown to other areas
under the sovereign's control.[35] In the end, resisting Justice Antonin
Scalia's prediction that its decision would have a "potentially harmful
effect upon the Nation's conduct of a war," the Court acted to protect
the civil liberties of citizens and noncitizens alike.[36]

Finally, while the Court's holding in *Rumsfeld v. Padilla* is
superficially the most progovernment of the three, it too differs from
decisions like *Abrams* and *Korematsu*. In *Padilla*, the Court agreed
with the government that a district court in New York lacked jurisdiction over Jose Padilla because the habeas statute requires a
detainee to sue his immediate custodian. The Court did not uphold

33. *Rasul v. Bush*, 124 S. Ct. 2686, 2696 (2004).
34. *Id.*
35. *Id.* at 2696–97.
36. *Id.* at 2710 (Scalia, J., dissenting). The *Rasul* majority opinion, if it is interpreted broadly, may reach much farther than Guantanamo Bay. In fact, Justice
Scalia's sharp dissent suggested that the Court's interpretation of the habeas statute
would apply to military detainees in Afghanistan and Iraq. It remains to be seen
whether this statutory jurisdiction extends to those held on American bases overseas
or even to occupied territories. Even without that extension, however, it seems safe
to say that this decision does not follow the patterns of past crisis jurisprudence.

the constitutionality of Padilla's detention; its opinion simply required Padilla to refile his petition in South Carolina. Although *Padilla* postponed the ultimate consideration of executive authority and due process, it seems certain that *at least* the logic of *Hamdi* will one day be applied to the circumstances of this case. This suggests that the government's victory in *Padilla* is likely to be short-lived. Any judicial surrender to executive prerogatives found in this jurisdictional holding cannot compare with the examples from the 1790s, 1860s, 1910s, or the 1940s.

What, then, explains the disjunction between the recent terrorism cases and the historical patterns that Justice Brennan and Chief Justice Rehnquist and others have observed? I offer four considerations.

1. One explanation draws on the work of Mark Tushnet and David Cole. In different ways, these scholars have proposed that repeated experience with the cycle can affect the way courts act during later iterations. Justice Brennan grounded the cycle on the fact that the United States had only faced episodic security threats for much of its history. As a result, he believed, decision makers, including judges, tended to get swept away by irrational fears and lacked the experience or expertise to critically evaluate executive claims of necessity. Tushnet and Cole's works encourage us to consider how the accumulation of knowledge from past cycles might affect judges in the present day.

Professor Tushnet wrote about the influence of social learning on our contemporary understandings of crises.[37] He suggested that lessons of history can tacitly shape contemporary actions. For instance, if we recognize that officials have exaggerated threats in the past or if we now believe that the courts were once mistaken, we may learn to become progressively more critical when confronted with the

---

37. Mark Tushnet, *Defending* Korematsu?: *Reflections on Civil Liberties in Wartime*, 2000 WIS. L. REV. 273 (2000).

next crisis. This hindsight wisdom thereby adjusts our *current* understandings of the balance between civil liberties and national security,
even when we are still in the crisis phase of a cycle.

Tushnet discussed how the current universal condemnation of
Korematsu might have influenced some of the actions, if not the legal
arguments, that the Bush administration has pursued. This process of
social learning might actually apply with greater force to judges.
Supreme Court justices, like any other human beings, look back and
learn from the Court's mistakes. They care about their reputations
today and how history will remember them tomorrow. They are held
to a higher standard, precisely because they are seen as being most
responsible for protecting civil liberties. In these recent cases, then,
the Supreme Court may have internalized the widely accepted legal
and cultural norm that they must avoid another *Korematsu*. The
Court's statement in *Hamdi* that "history and common sense teach
us that an unchecked system of detention carries the potential to
become a means for oppression and abuse of others who do not present that sort of threat" supports this view.[38]

David Cole made a related argument.[39] He contended that current descriptions of the cycle underestimate the prospective legal
impact of the decisions made after the crisis has ended. He argued
that the precedential authority of decisions that may have "come too
late" can nonetheless set the legal terms for the future. Cases like
Milligan, Duncan, and *Brandenburg* impose important limits on the
government and courts during the *next* crisis, even if they failed to
do so in the preceding one. According to Professor Cole, the common-law method is especially conducive to placing restraints on
future courts. Over time, the requirement that judges write opinions
and give reasons can serve to restrain the worst violations of civil

38. *Hamdi,* 124 S. Ct. at 2697.
39. David Cole, *Symposium: Judging Judicial Review:* Marbury *in the Modern
Era: Judging the Next Emergency: Judicial Review and Individual Rights in Times of
Crisis,* 101 MICH. L. REV. 2565, 2571–77 (2003).

liberties during the next emergency. Cole, then, encouraged us to take a long view of crisis jurisprudence and to examine the ways in which decisions made in one cycle may influence the next.

The three terrorism decisions offer some support for Coles's thesis. Decisions such as *Milligan* and even *Braden v. 30th Judicial Circuit of Kentucky*—on which the *Rasul* Court relied to distinguish *Eisentrager*—were used at key points in the combatant detention opinions to support the Court's most rights-protective conclusions. The dissenters also discussed these peacetime decisions extensively, and the plurality was forced to address their arguments in its own opinion. What is more, we may never be able to know the extent to which *uncited* decisions nevertheless exerted a subtle influence on the justices in these cases, providing important boundaries for their reasoning even though they did not appear in the actual opinions.

2. A second possible reason why the terrorism cases do not fit neatly within the cycle is something I would call "the Israeli explanation." In contrast to the American experience of *episodic* exposure to national security threats, Israel has faced nearly continuous threats for as long as it has existed. Unlike their American counterparts, Israeli judges have experienced the need to act in a context of a crisis seemingly without end. And by and large their developed jurisprudence is substantially more rights-protective than are U.S. wartime decisions.

Living in a state of never-ending threat—and perhaps also having all served in the military—Israeli judges have been far less inclined to accept at face value claims of national security necessity. For example, in 1999, the Israeli Supreme Court barred the Israeli Security Services from using certain physical interrogation techniques, such as sleep deprivation or "shak[ing]."[40] Similarly, that court decided a case in the spring of 2004 dealing with the military's procedures for detaining "unlawful combatants" in the West Bank. Regulations spec-

40. H.C.J. 500/94, *Public Comm. Against Torture v. Israel*, 1999 ISR. L. REPORTS 1, 38 (Sept. 9, 1999).

ified that the army could detain alleged combatants without judicial
review or access to counsel for up to eighteen days and could delay
its investigation of the detainees for up to eight days. The court found
this period to be too long. It stated that "delays must not exceed a
few days" and that even an unlawful combatant "is to be brought
promptly before a judge." The Court struck down the eight-day wait-
ing period for investigations, holding that they must begin immediately. It held that counsel must be provided after four days, unless a
case-by-case analysis determined that further delay was necessary.[41]
On balance, this ruling provided strong safeguards for civil liberties—
far stronger, in fact, than those found in the U.S. Supreme Court's
combatant detention decisions.[42]

In his 2002 *Harvard Law Review* foreword, Israeli Chief Justice
Aharon Barak explained the approach that animates these decisions.
Dismissing any possibility of cyclical behavior, he wrote that in Israel,

> [t]he line between war and peace is thin—what one person calls
> peace, another calls war. In any case, it is impossible to maintain
> this distinction over the long term. Since its founding, Israel has
> faced a security threat. As a Justice of the Israeli Supreme Court,
> how should I view my role in protecting human rights given this
> situation? I must take human rights seriously during times of both
> peace and conflict. I must not make do with the mistaken belief
> that, at the end of the conflict, I can turn back the clock.[43]

41. H.C. 3239/02, *Marab v. IDF Commander in the W. Bank*, 57(2) P.D. 349
(2003).
42. The Israeli Supreme Court's recent decision on the "separation fence" is
another example of Israeli courts upholding human rights in the face of executive
claims of national security necessity. The Court ordered the Israeli army to remove
a twenty-mile portion of the security fence and to reroute other sections to minimize
the harms imposed on Palestinians. The Court explicitly acknowledged that the
decision might make it easier for terrorists to attack Israel, but it also confidently
stated that "[s]atisfying the provisions of the law is an aspect of national security."
Dan Izenberg, *High Court Rejects Security Fence Route*, JERUSALEM POST, Jun. 28,
2004, at 1.
43. Aharon Barak, A Judge on Judging: The Role of a Supreme Court in a Democracy, 116 HARV. L. REV. 16, 149 (2002).

Since there is no opportunity for post hoc correction in Israel, Barak went on to say, the basic struggle for a judge is to always preserve the proper balance between national security and the freedom of the individual.

Although it has been only three years since September 11, it is worth considering whether the justices of the U.S. Supreme Court have developed an outlook similar to Justice Barak's. The *Hamdi* plurality opinion clearly recognized that the war with al Qaeda and similar groups was an "unconventional war" that might last for more than a generation. The Court, for example, cited the government's concession that this was not a war that would end with a formal cease-fire. Justice O'Connor specifically stated that "the national security underpinnings of the 'war on terror,' although crucially important, are broad and malleable."[44] It is possible, then, that the nature of the war on terror affected the outcomes of these cases. Under these new conditions, the Court may have internalized Justice Barak's belief that long-lasting conflicts deprive courts of the "luxuries" of the Brennan/Rehnquist cycle. Perhaps America's experience with a war on terror has compelled its law to look a bit more like Israel's.

3. So far, I have assumed that in June 2004 we were still in an active phase of the war on terror. But a third potential explanation why the combatant detention decisions do not look like classic mid-crisis decisions is that the justices may have perceived that we have moved beyond that point in the cycle. I think it is likely that the three decisions handed down on June 28, 2004, would have looked quite different had they been announced on September 20, 2001. The passage of time has unquestionably altered public perceptions of both the threat and the necessary government response. In the intervening years, Americans, including the members of the Court, may have become more accustomed to the persistent threats posed by Islamic terrorism. The inevitably prolonged and inchoate nature of the war

44. *Hamdi*, 124 S. Ct. at 2641.

on terror—coupled with the fact that there have been no follow-up
attacks on the U.S. homeland since September 11—differentiates it
from past crises like the Civil War or World War II. Though the war
on terror is still active and dangerous, it is also not continuously
apparent to most Americans. There is no draft, no nationwide food
rationing, and we no longer see many yellow ribbons hanging on
trees across suburban America. Life has simply gone on despite the
al Qaeda threat. As such, the ever-present risk of attack and the constant stream of alerts—or what the *New York Times* once called "the
ill-explained upswing[s] of the government's yellow-orange yo-yo of
terror warnings"[45]—might have changed the common perception of
where we are in this crisis. This adjustment might well have influenced the justices' approach to these cases. Although the crisis is
ongoing—and indeed *Hamdi* is predicated on the continuation of
military operations in Afghanistan—the Court may have offered these
more balanced opinions because it perceived itself to be in a different
part of the cycle: somewhere in between war and peace or security
and insecurity. In this respect, the cycle may have worked just as
Justice Brennan or Chief Justice Rehnquist would have predicted.
The Court's adoption of the *Mathews* balancing paradigm may permit future courts to institutionalize this sensitivity to the varying
national security exigencies as the nature of the crisis evolves.

4. On the other hand, a final explanation of why the combatant
detention decisions defy the expectations of the cycle is that the cycle
was never really an accurate description of history in the first place.
The historical examples I discussed earlier—drawing on the descriptions offered by Justice Brennan and Chief Justice Rehnquist—are
highly stylized. In discussing the Civil War, for example, I neglected
to address *Ex Parte Merryman*, in which Chief Justice Roger Taney,
sitting on circuit, ruled that President Lincoln had no authority to

45. Todd S. Purdum, *What, Us Worry? The New State of Disbelief*, N.Y. TIMES,
Aug. 8, 2004, § 4, at 1.

unilaterally suspend the writ of habeas corpus. *Merryman* was decided in 1861, when the crisis of disunion was urgent. The case is largely remembered today for Lincoln's refusal to abide by Taney's holding, but it can also serve as an example of judicial respect for civil liberties in times of war.

Similarly, the standard account of World War II legal history strangely overlooks a decision, handed down the same day as *Korematsu*, that cut an important leg from under the government's internment policy. In *Ex parte Endo*, the petitioner, a U.S. citizen, had been removed to a relocation center in Utah under the terms of the Japanese exclusion order. She filed a habeas corpus petition, claiming that she was a loyal and law-abiding citizen, that no charge had been made against her, and that she was being detained against her will. The government conceded all of these facts, and the Court found that the government had no right to hold citizens who were concededly loyal.[46] It was a narrow holding, but it was also one that clearly defies the historical pattern. As one scholar, Patrick O. Gudridge, wrote, "*Endo* closed the camps. Why don't we remember *Endo*?"[47]

There are many possible answers to Gudridge's question, but I offer two final thoughts in connection with the cycle. First, Justice Brennan's important insight about the episodic nature of crises in American history may be as damning as it is causal. Famous or infamous decisions like *Milligan* and *Korematsu* tend to overshadow ones like *Endo* and *Merryman*. Likewise, problematic wartime decisions like *Quirin* and *Abrams* can eclipse the quiet protections that take place in more continuing crises like the Cold War. In this regard, both the salience and the small sample size of crisis jurisprudence might allow the worst mistakes to stand out too noticeably and to overdetermine the historical model. The danger of describing history

46. *Ex parte Endo*, 323 U.S. 283 (1944).
47. Patrick O. Gudridge, *Remember Endo?* 116 HARV. L. REV. 1933, 1934 (2003).

with simple models is that a few examples will simply be used to prove too much.

Second, modern proponents of the cycle thesis generally rely on *Korematsu* as *the* emblematic decision.[48] I suggest that we might forget *Endo* for the same reasons that the cycle theory may have been developed in the first place—perhaps the cycle theory operates as an apology for *Korematsu*—a case that, like *Dred Scott, Plessy,* and *Lochner* "has come to live in infamy."[49] But unlike those other three blunders, *Korematsu* may be more easily categorized into a fancy theoretical model, like the crisis cycle; this model, then, can serve as a convenient, guilty explanation for one of the Court's most egregious errors. If this is true, it would be wrong to view the past—*and the present*—through a cycle built around *Korematsu.*

Certainly, centuries of American history cannot easily be reconciled by a single overarching theory. There are too many nuances and counterexamples for a paradigm like the cycle to perfectly describe the broad strokes of history and law. *Hamdi, Padilla,* and *Rasul* may just be the most recent evidence of this—and of how the cycle may not neatly capture the broad strokes of American history. Yet of the four explanations I have offered, I am inclined to credit some combination of the first three and largely to reject the fourth. The cycle described by Justice Brennan and Chief Justice Rehnquist is far too robust a phenomenon—both theoretical and historical—to jettison simply because the combatant detention cases (and some others) do not readily fit. Far more likely, courts have learned from the nation's cyclical precedents and understand, as do Israeli courts, that

---

48. *See* REHNQUIST; MARTIN S. SHEFFER, THE JUDICIAL DEVELOPMENT OF PRESIDENTIAL WAR POWERS (1999); Joel B. Grossman, *The Japanese American Cases and the Vagaries of Constitutional Adjudication in Wartime: An Institutional Perspective,* 19 U. HAW. L. REV. 649 (1997); Brennan, at 16–17; Lee Epstein et al., *The Effect of War on the U.S. Supreme Court,* at http://gkind.Harvard.edu/files/crisis.pdf.

49. KATHLEEN M. SULLIVAN & GERALD GUNTHER, CONSTITUTIONAL LAW 631 n. 4 (14th ed. 2001).

a war without end requires a more refined response to urgent claims of national security.

II.

I began with Justice O'Connor's statement in *Hamdi*—that the courts are capable of properly balancing civil liberties and national security—in order to place the combatant detention decisions in the debate over how well the Court has carried out that balancing in the past.[50] But Justice O'Connor's statement also points to another context in which to view the combatant detention decisions: the growth of the Court's confidence in its capacity as a social policy maker in many realms since World War II. Indeed, in his dissent, Justice Scalia commented derisively on this aspect of the *Hamdi* plurality opinion:

> There is a certain harmony of approach in the plurality's making up for Congress's failure to invoke the Suspension Clause and its making up for the Executive's failure to apply what it says are needed procedures—an approach that reflects what might be called a Mr. Fix-it Mentality. The plurality seems to view it as its mission to Make Everything Come Out Right, rather than merely to decree the consequences, as far as individual rights are concerned, of the other two branches' actions and omissions. . . . The problem with this approach is not only that it steps out of the courts' modest and limited role in a democratic society; but that by repeatedly doing what it thinks the political branches ought to do it encourages their lassitude and saps the vitality of government by the people.[51]

While Justice Scalia probably overstated the extent to which the Court usurped the role of the political branches, there is no denying that the current Court is more muscular in its relations with the political branches than it has been for a long time.

50. *Hamdi*, 124 S. Ct. at 2652.
51. *Id.* at 2673 (Scalia, J., dissenting).

Perhaps it is this confidence, this "Mr. Fix-it Mentality," and not any exogenous cycle, that best explains the Court's approach to the detainee cases. As the Court's view of itself as an institution has evolved over time, perhaps these changes have influenced its treatment of civil liberties in general, including its wartime civil liberties perspective. Accordingly, it might be helpful to look at the detainee decisions through the broader lens of interbranch relations rather than the limited perspective of crisis jurisprudence. I do so below (although in somewhat less detail than the previous section, since several of the other contributors to this volume also touch on this point).

Of course, the powerful, confident Court we see today was not created in a day. For much of its early history, this "least dangerous branch"[52] faced the real threat that the executive branch would fail to enforce the Court's decisions. For example, while the Court's decision in *Ex parte Milligan* was honored by the executive, earlier in the war, the chief justice, sitting on circuit, had issued a similar challenge to the executive's authority in *Ex parte Merryman* and was ignored. Likewise, just a few decades earlier, the Court took a strong stand in *Worcester v. Georgia* (the Cherokee Indians case), and the president refused to enforce its decision.

Even into the late nineteenth century, the Court often avoided direct confrontations with the executive, likely expecting that the Court would emerge the weaker from any such clash. Indeed, the Court has historically been far more deferential than the current Court to presidential claims of broad powers inherent in that office. In *In re Neagle*, for example, decided in 1890, the Court upheld the actions of the attorney general in appointing a bodyguard to protect a Supreme Court justice, despite the absence of explicit congressional delegation of this power. The Court held that the president's authority

---

52. The Federalist, no. 78 (noting that the judiciary wielded neither the sword nor the purse).

to take care that the laws are faithfully executed must apply not only to acts of Congress but also to the "rights, duties and obligations growing out of the Constitution itself, our international relations, and all the protection implied by the nature of the government under the Constitution."[53]

Likewise, in *In re Debs*, a case arising out of the Pullman Strike of 1894, the attorney general sought to enjoin labor leaders from interfering with the functioning of the railroads, which in turn disrupted delivery of the mail. A federal court held that the labor leaders had violated the Sherman Act and issued an injunction on that basis. Although the Court ignored the Sherman Act claims, the majority upheld the legality of the injunction, even in the absence of explicit statutory authorization, apparently acknowledging that seeking the injunction was within the executive's implied powers.

Similarly, in the early years of Franklin Roosevelt's first administration, the Supreme Court under Charles Evans Hughes clashed with the president over a number of New Deal enactments, declaring them unconstitutional at an unprecedented rate. But Roosevelt ultimately prevailed: In a "switch in time that saved nine," Justice Owen Roberts changed his vote in *West Coast Hotel Co. v. Parrish*, effectively shifting the ideological balance of the Court in favor of Roosevelt's programs.

Early traces of the current Court's institutional self-confidence can be traced in several domains. In the area of national security cases, consensus places *Youngstown Sheet & Tube v. Sawyer* at the apex of the judiciary's power vis-à-vis the executive branch. In the days leading up to that case, negotiations between labor and management in the steel industry broke down, and work stoppages loomed. President Harry Truman, concerned that a halt in steel production would impair his ability to successfully wage war in Korea, seized the steel mills by executive order. The owners of the steel mills

53. *In re Neagle*, 135 U.S. 1, 64 (1890).

responded rapidly, seeking injunctive relief in the federal courts. The Supreme Court ultimately sided with the steel mills, holding that Truman lacked both the statutory and the constitutional authority to seize the mills.

Given the Court's cabining of executive power in *Youngstown* more than fifty years ago, the combatant detention decisions may seem less surprising. But although *Youngstown* may look like a risky confrontation for the Court, evidence suggests that the petitioners had public opinion overwhelmingly on their side. The *Chicago Daily News* described the seizure as an example of socialism in action.[54] Likewise, the *New York Daily News* declared that "Hitler and Mussolini would have loved this."[55] The *Washington Post* opined that "President Truman's seizure of the steel industry will probably go down in history as one of the most high-handed acts committed by an American President."[56] Even President Truman's own Justice Department recommended against the seizure. Thus, the Court could confidently confront the executive, secure in the knowledge that the public would support them. The same was not true in *Korematsu* or in the combatant detention cases.

In their defiance of a considerable segment of public opinion, the civil rights decisions that followed shortly after *Youngstown* are probably better examples of the emergence of a more confident Supreme Court. As we mark the fiftieth anniversary of *Brown v. Board of Education*, a number of commentators have emphasized the limits of *Brown*'s impact. But it is important to remember the formidable task the Court saw itself taking on in *Brown*, overseeing a process that would fundamentally restructure Southern society and precipitating nothing less than a social and political revolution. That the Court believed itself capable of achieving the desegregation of public edu-

54. *See President Truman and the Steel Seizure Case: A 50-Year Retrospective*, 41 Duǫ. L. Rev. 685, 690 (2003).
55. *Id.*
56. *Id.*

cation reflects no little confidence in its own capabilities. And although the Supreme Court under Chief Justices Burger and Rehnquist has retreated from some of the Warren Court's civil rights decisions, it has most often done so not out of judicial reticence but as a result of a different view of substantive law.

Indeed, despite their disagreement with some of the Warren Court's results, the Burger and Rehnquist Courts have been institutional beneficiaries of the former's civil rights and individual rights trailblazing. Those rights-expanding decisions helped elevate the modern Court's stature in the eyes of the legal community and of the broader public. This, in turn, has provided the Court with greater reservoirs of authority as it confronts new issues. For those who applaud the Court's exercise of authority, a virtuous cycle has been at work. Americans cherish their right to speak freely, for example, and their right to be free from discrimination based on race, ethnicity, religion, and gender. Americans expect to be accorded due process, to be protected from governmental intrusion on their privacy, and to have a say in how their government is run. As these rights have become articles of secular faith, the institution charged with protecting them has gained in stature. The Court has reason to be self-confident.

Evidence of this confidence can be found in the Court's accelerating willingness to strike down acts of Congress. Between 1995 and 2002, the Court struck down thirty-three federal laws, an average of more than four a year. By contrast, only 134 acts of Congress were overturned in the 206 years between 1789 and 1995.[57] Even more remarkable than the sheer number of laws the current Court has struck down is the fact that almost half (fifteen) of these decisions were products of five-vote majorities. Of the 134 decisions invalidating statutes prior to 1995, only twenty-two were rendered by a bare

57. Jed Handelsman Shugerman, *A Six-Three Rule: Reviving Consensus and Deference on the Supreme Court*, 37 GA. L. REV. 893 (2003).

majority of justices. And while "few of the five–four decisions before 1995 are considered major precedents,"[58] several of the more recent 5–4 decisions clearly are. These include *Board of Trustees of the University of Alabama v. Garrett, Alden v. Maine, Seminole Tribe v. Florida, United States v. Lopez, United States v. Morrison,* and *Printz v. United States.*[59]

A similar attitude among the justices is evident in the Court's recent political-question jurisprudence. Questions that previous Supreme Courts treated as political—as within the discretion of the political branches—appear to be increasingly viewed by the current Court as justiciable, providing only (and only occasionally) deference to the interpretations of the political branches in these matters.[60]

Many of the Court's more recent separation of powers cases also reflect heightened institutional confidence. The Court has reigned in the executive branch in cases such as *Clinton v. New York* and *Clinton v. Jones,* and it has held that Congress improperly aggrandized its power in cases such as *Bowsher v. Synar, INS v. Chadha, Metropolitan Washington Airports Authority v. Citizens for the Abatement of Aircraft Noise, Inc.,* and perhaps most notably *City of Boerne v. Flores.* Justice O'Connor emphasized the importance of the Court's role in maintaining the separation of powers in her *Hamdi* plurality opinion: "Whatever power the United States Constitution envisions for the Executive in its exchanges with other nations or with enemy organi-

---

58. *Id.*

59. Not all of these 5–4 decisions striking down statutes can be ascribed solely, or even principally, to a particular ideological tilt to the current Court. While eleven of the fifteen 5–4 decisions mentioned here included the five more conservative justices in the majority, the so-called "liberals" on the Court also managed to put together five-vote majorities to strike down statutes. As much as anything, the Court's recent inclination to strike down acts of Congress reflects a new confidence on the Court that straddles lines of both ideology and judicial philosophy.

60. See, e.g., *Bush v. Gore,* 531 U.S. 98 (2000); *United States v. Munoz-Flores,* 495 U.S. 385 (1990); *Japan Whaling Ass'n v. American Cetacean Society,* 478 U.S. 221 (1986).

zations in times of conflict, it most assuredly envisions a role for all three branches when individual liberties are at stake."[61]

Yet although this is a powerful Court, it is also one that customarily favors restraint in the scope of its decisions. At the same time that the Court boldly strikes down acts of Congress, it often seems intensely aware of the need to keep each decision limited to the particular, often narrowly crafted, question presented and to postpone consideration of related questions until future cases. A minimalist strategy recognizing rights in resolving the case immediately before it, but leaving the content of the remedy vague, may also have the virtue of encouraging the political branches to help craft a solution, taking advantage of the political branches' superior institutional competencies.

Both the Court's institutional confidence and its minimalist tendencies are evident in the detainee decisions. Certainly, *Padilla* was about as minimalist a decision as one is ever likely to find.[62] By deciding the case on procedural grounds, the majority put off resolving the status of American citizens captured within the United States and designated as enemy combatants—permitting, and perhaps encouraging, a national conversation on this bedrock question.

The resolution of *Hamdi* is also minimalist in important ways. The plurality did explicitly indicate that citizens detained as enemy combatants in the Afghan war are entitled to the rudiments of due process—that "[a] state of war is not a blank check for the President when it comes to the rights of the nation's citizens."[63] But in declining to outline precisely the contours of due process for American citizens held as enemy combatants, the plurality also reserved flexibility for the executive branch. Americans, for example, may yet be tried by military tribunals. The Court may define the required pro-

61. *Hamdi*, 124 S. Ct. at 2650.
62. Cass R. Sunstein, *The Smallest Court in the Land*, NEW YORK TIMES, July 4, 2004, § 4 at 9.
63. *Hamdi*, 124 S. Ct. at 2650, citing *Youngstown*.

cedures with greater specificity when these cases are next appealed, but for now the Court has accorded the political branches some room to maneuver.

Rasul is more difficult to characterize as "minimalist" in any classic sense. The majority opinion is broader than Justice Kennedy's concurrence, which predicated jurisdiction on narrow grounds; also, in recognizing a statutory basis for jurisdiction, the Court may well have extended access to the federal courts well beyond Guantanamo Bay. But was *Rasul*, as Justice Scalia suggested in dissent, "judicial adventurism of the worst sort"?[64] To be sure, that decision reflects the workings of a muscular, self-confident Court. But it also reflects a Court operating within its core competency—defining the basic rights and obligations of parties under the Constitution. In both *Rasul* and *Hamdi*, the Court sought to assert its view of the appropriate separation of powers, as it has in so many other recent decisions.

In a way, the very ambiguity that characterizes this aspect of the *Rasul* decision is likely to achieve the goals minimalists espouse: The decision gives the executive branch another chance to choose a more sensible course of action, and it invites Congress to enter the fray.[65] Among other things, *Rasul* has almost nothing to say about the standards that will govern the merits stage of the litigation; the parties continue, for example, to spar over whether the detainees are entitled to have access to lawyers based on *Rasul* and *Hamdi* taken together.

Some might argue that it reflects institutional timidity for a Court that could plainly have reached further to decline to do so. That seems quite a mistaken view of this Court, especially in these cases. Here, as in *Marbury v. Madison*, judicial restraint betokens institutional strength. In the combatant detention cases, the Court demonstrated that it has an integral role to play in the constitutional

64. *Rasul*, 124 S. Ct. at 2711.

65. As John Hart Ely explained in WAR AND RESPONSIBILITY 47–67 (1993), there is considerable reason to doubt that Congress will eagerly seize the Court's invitation to become involved.

order and that it is the final arbiter of what the Constitution (including the Commander-in-Chief Clause) allows. Yet the Court also recognized its own limitations. It acknowledged that it cannot perform fact-finding functions and make policy decisions as well, or as legitimately, as do the political branches. To my mind, the combatant detention decisions enhanced the Court's stature and ensured that whatever next steps the executive (and perhaps Congress) takes, those steps will be brought before the Court for renewed scrutiny.

III.

Drawing on the work of many fine scholars and jurists, I have tried to gauge the significance of the combatant detention cases by viewing them through two alternative historical lenses: the Court's episodic confrontations with civil liberties questions during periods of national security crisis and the rise in recent decades of the Court's institutional power vis-à-vis the other branches of the federal government that is visible across a range of issues unrelated to national security. But, of course, neither of these lenses offers a complete or crystal-clear view. Indeed, we are still so close to the decisions that much about their ultimate significance remains undetermined. I'd like to close by briefly mentioning two sources of that indeterminacy.

First, we don't yet know conclusively how the executive branch and Congress will respond to the decisions. Those responses will do much to shape the practical consequences of the decisions.

So far, the executive branch seems to be following a policy of minimal compliance. Rather than giving Yaser Hamdi the process mandated by the Court, the military has let him go—perhaps in significant part to prevent the Court from having an opportunity to say more precisely how much process he was due. In the Guantanamo cases, the government has read the Court's decision extremely narrowly, insisting in filings before the district court on remand that (1) the petitioners do not have a right to meet with counsel to discuss the habeas petitions the Supreme Court has now said the federal courts possess the jurisdiction to hear and (2) the petitions should still be dismissed on the pleadings because aliens captured and held outside the United States, even innocent ones, have absolutely no legal rights (notwithstanding the apparent conclusion in the *Rasul* decision to the contrary[66]).

Congress has yet to react at all, but the decisions leave open an array of possibilities. Congress may, according to the *Hamdi* plurality, either broaden or narrow the president's power to detain citizen enemy combatants. For example, rather than limiting the president's authorization to use force in Afghanistan or Iraq, perhaps Congress could authorize more limited actions but with a broader geographic reach. Presumably, in future authorizations for the use of force, Congress could also specify that it is not delegating the power to detain American citizens to the president. With respect to noncitizen detainees, a number of responses are also available to Congress. If the statutory basis of jurisdiction recognized in *Rasul* ends up being as broad as some suggest, Congress could amend the habeas corpus statute to ensure that it does not reach beyond Guantanamo. If Congress wants to allow the military to continue to detain combatants at Guantanamo without complying with the procedural requirements demanded by *Rasul*, it could formally suspend the writ of habeas corpus for that area.[67] Congress could also attempt to strip federal courts of jurisdiction to review habeas petitions originating outside the territory of the United States, or at least raise the bar for invoking the writ.[68]

66. *Rasul*, 124 S. Ct. at 2698 & n.15.
67. Of course, Article I, § 9, of the Constitution permits suspension of the writ only "when in Cases of Rebellion or Invasion the public Safety may require it." But Congress might determine that the threat from al Qaeda constitutes an invasion—a determination that may be plausible when operatives whose actions threaten the functioning of the government are arrested within the United States.
68. Jurisdiction stripping conflicts with aggressive interpretations of *Marbury v. Madison* might even be argued to constitute a suspension of the writ, in which case Congress's action would be subject to the same conditions that would attend a more

Congress may also cabin executive discretion in this area by designing procedures for the military to employ in determining whether to continue holding detainees. It could even compose a War Powers Resolution for the new era of the war on terror.

If the president and Congress may yet reshape our understanding of the combatant detention decisions, the courts themselves may also. Using the example of *United States v. Nixon*, the presidential tapes case, Professor Vicki Jackson noted that when *Nixon* was decided, most observers viewed the decision as a victory for strong limitations on the powers of the executive. But because the decision formally recognized a constitutional doctrine of executive privilege, *Nixon* over time has come to be seen as the foundational case for assertions of a special presidential entitlement to secrecy.[69] In fact, just last term, in *Cheney v. United States District Court*, the case concerning the records of the President's Energy Policy Task Force, the Supreme Court quoted *Nixon* in stating: "'A President's communications and activities encompass a vastly wider range of sensitive material than would be true of any "ordinary individual."'" The Court explained that while "the president is [not] above the law," the judiciary must "'afford Presidential confidentiality the greatest possible protection,'" recognizing "the paramount necessity of protecting the Executive Branch from vexatious litigation that might distract it from the energetic performance of its constitutional duties."[70] What was originally understood as a holding that restricts executive power has now become one that buttresses it. One could well imagine a similar transformation in our appreciation of the terrorism decisions. Initially, *Hamdi* has been seen as a loss for presidential power. But as in the

---

straightforward suspension. On the other hand, we know from *Turpin v. Felker* that merely raising the bar for those who hope to qualify for habeas relief does not violate the Exceptions Clause or constitute a suspension of the writ.

69. Vicki C. Jackson, *Being Proportional About Proportionality: A Review of David Beatty's* The Ultimate Rule of Law, Constitutional Commentary, n.168 (forthcoming, 2005).

70. *Cheney v. United States District Court*, 124 S. Ct. 2587–88.

Nixon decision, *Hamdi* and the other combatant detention decisions affixed the Court's imprimatur to a legal category that previously had been of uncertain standing. However limited the category "enemy combatant" may be at the moment, the *Hamdi* Court undoubtedly gave it new legal status, and it could one day be applied far more expansively.

The combatant detention trilogy's ultimate impact, then, is far from clear. However, as we face the prospect of a war against Islamic fundamentalist groups extending many years into the future, the Court's ringing declaration that "[i]t is during our most challenging and uncertain moments that . . . we must preserve our commitment at home to the principles for which we fight abroad,"[71] sends an important signal at the outset of a lengthy period of threat that the judiciary will play an important role in guarding those principles upon which we all depend.

---

71. *Hamdi*, 124 S. Ct. at 2648.

2. The Supreme Court Goes to War

Patricia M. Wald

1. Did the Court Wade in Too Far?

In his colorful dissent in *Hamdi v. Rumsfeld*, one of the three enemy combatant cases decided at the end of the 2004 term, Justice Antonin Scalia accused the plurality opinion of "what might be called a Mr. Fix-it Mentality."[1] According to Scalia, "The plurality seems to view it as its mission to Make Everything Come Out Right, rather than merely to decree the consequences, as far as individual rights are concerned, of the other two branches' actions and omissions." This conceit, in his view, has consequences for Congress and the president: "[This approach] encourages their lassitude and saps the vitality of government by the people."

For decades, a political and academic debate has been waged over the appropriate role of the judiciary in the complex social, economic, and moral issues of our national life. At year 2004, add war to that mix. All such issues, of course, have serious legal questions, attached like barnacles to their bodies corpora. So is it enough, then,

---

1. *Hamdi v. Rumsfeld*, 124 S. Ct. 2633, 2673 (2004).

for the Court to locate the legal issue, decide it, and let the other branches of government and societal groups deal with untoward consequences and devise solutions? In the past, this has been the query commentators have asked after the Court's pronouncements on abortion, affirmative action, separation of church and state, gay rights, and the like. But in 2004, this query was raised in the heretofore sacrosanct sphere of war and foreign relations, long regarded as an executive bastion. Like Justice Scalia, some critics of the enemy combatant decisions view the Court, in at least two of the cases, as acting as a superlegislature, putting its own fix on complicated areas formerly left to diplomacy and military judgment. But is that critique fair? Has the Court crossed a bridge too far in telling the other branches, schooled in the conduct of war, what to do and how to do it? Or, as other critics assert, has the Court, in effect, taken on the role of the Music Man, leading the parade, with the seventy-six trombones of our policy-making apparatus straggling behind? Opinions vary. This chapter will attempt to tease out the implications of the Court's several pronouncements for those policy makers and to suggest the unanswered questions that may require a second look by the Court itself.

There is, of course, a basic difference between the enemy combatant cases and earlier hot-button issues where the Court's intervention proved especially controversial. The enemy combatant cases did not involve issues of federalism where fifty "laboratory" states might be working independently on local solutions and competing for best answers. The federal government's jurisdiction over treatment of captured combatants was exclusive. Nor was this an issue that the other two branches had steadfastly refused to take on, such as racial segregation. In this case, the executive branch had seized the reins with vengeance and warned the others away, including, notably, the judiciary. In fact, apart from its September 19, 2001, resolution authorizing "necessary and appropriate force" against those involved with or harboring 9/11 terrorists, Congress had made no attempt to legislate or even hold hearings as to what should be done with such persons after their capture. The status and treatment of so-called enemy combatants were solely at the executive's discretion or whim. Apart from a few "most favored nation" bows to our allies who had a handful of citizens among the more than 600 prisoners held at Guantanamo Bay, no known diplomatic initiatives had been undertaken. The executive was doing its thing without outside intervention of any kind from any other authority.

But what the *Washington Post* called "international opprobrium"[2] rained down on the United States for its alleged flaunting of international human rights and the laws of war. Front-page color photographs of hooded, shackled, caged prisoners being held incommunicado on the U.S. Guantanamo Base in Cuba for an indefinite duration, with no access to families, press, or lawyers and interminably subjected to interrogations conducted without the protections of the Geneva Conventions, repelled not only allies and enemies abroad but also many of our own citizens. The mainline press here and abroad sided with the American Bar Association, Amnesty International, Human Rights Watch, and scores of civil liberties and human rights groups to protest the status and conditions of the detainees. Even the Red Cross uncharacteristically went public with criticism of the detainees' treatment. When it was revealed that not only foreigners but also American citizens held inside the United States were being treated similarly, the clamor rose to sufficient heights that something had to give. In the United States, the situation inevitably spawned lawsuits. Despite the logistic obstacles to representing incarcerated clients who did not even know that they had lawyers or that lawsuits had been brought on their behalf and who until after, or just before, the Supreme Court heard their cases never got to see or talk to anyone about their legal rights, a half dozen habeas corpus suits were filed and lurched their way up to the Supreme Court.

2. *Belated Reform* (ed.), Wash. Post, July 9, 2004, at A18.

No one could block the lawsuits from being filed, of course, but the Supreme Court could and, it was widely predicted, *would* make short shrift of them by denials of certiorari, particularly in the case of the foreign combatants housed at Guantanamo. An intact precedent from 1950, *Johnson v. Eisentrager*,[3] denied all recourse to U.S. courts for German citizens convicted of war crimes in a U.S. military tribunal abroad and held in an American prisoner of war camp in Germany. In fact, one of the two lower courts of appeal hearing the Guantanamo cases denied all relief and dismissed the writs on the basis of that earlier precedent.[4]

There were, however, perils in that course for the Supreme Court. One was the weak factual basis for ruling that the Guantanamo Naval Base, which operated on a ninety-nine-year renewable lease from Cuba, with the United States in total and exclusive control of everything on the base, was *not* U.S. territory and thus did not fall within the *Eisentrager* precedent (by the time the D.C. Circuit case reached the Supreme Court, the Ninth Circuit had already ruled that way).[5] Second, there was what was viewed by many as executive overreaching in claiming total secret and exclusive control over the detainees' fate, with no declared processes for review or ultimate release. *If* military review panels, which were already provided for in U.S. Army regulations implementing the Geneva Conventions, had been set up, as they had been in the Gulf and Vietnam Wars to hear prisoners' objections to their status as enemy combatants on the grounds that they were, in fact, innocent bystanders and were not engaged in combat alongside our enemies; and *if* the executive had announced a system of periodic reviews to determine whether prisoners could be safely released to their home countries (both of which procedures have been put in effect since the decision), there is at least a good chance the Court would not have waded in so far or

3. *Johnson v. Eisentrager*, 339 U.S. 763 (1950).
4. *Al Odah v. United States*, 321 F.2d 1134 (D.C. Cir. 2003).
5. *Gharebi v. Bush*, 352 F.2d 1278 (9th Cir. 2003).

chastised the executive so harshly. We can certainly speculate that had even those limited processes been in place, the Court might have said that an initial military hearing and periodic review procedures were enough for foreign-born prisoners captured on or near the battlefield, no matter where they were held, and that a full-press U.S. court habeas proceeding was not necessary, nor was there any precedent for its extension to this group. International humanitarian law, as expressed in the Geneva Conventions, would have supplied a sufficient validation for the executive's actions.

As it was, however, the government hung tough on the fifty-year-old *Eisentrager* precedent, which had been decided before the promulgation of the relevant Geneva Conventions on the treatment of battlefield captures, the European Convention on Human Rights, the International Covenant on Civil and Political Rights, and myriad judicial decisions from national, regional, and international courts condemning indefinite detention, even in wartime, without any judicial review (125 members of the British Parliament filed a brief on the prisoners' behalf in the Guantanamo cases). Although at the precise moment the cases were heard in the Supreme Court there were no published reports of torture or blatantly inhumane abuses of prisoners at Guatanamo, troubling rumors of long and harsh interrogations, denial of sleep, and bombardment by noise and bright lights were widespread. Most significantly, the despicable abuses at Abu Ghraib prison in Iraq exploded into the news on the very day of oral argument, only hours after the government lawyer defending the executive's treatment of Guantanamo prisoners had assured the Court that the United States did not engage in torture.

But perhaps, too, as eminent commentators observed, the Court's more interventionist stance was a "separation of powers thing." The Court would not be told by the executive it had no right to intervene in the treatment of battlefield detainees even though individual rights were at stake and prisoners were being held in total isolation for months and years without reference to any legal regime, national or international. The Court, when all is said and done, is a wily body (several of its members are avowed internationalists), and it is reasonable to believe that its members recognized our country, after 9/11, was involved in a new kind of war, with new dilemmas that needed new rules—the world was watching, and foreign critics were already pouncing on us as hypocrites for refusing to practice the rule-of-law values we preached so aggressively. Moreover, the Court had to be acutely aware of the infamous *Korematsu* decision, which upheld the executive's internment of 120,000 loyal Japanese Americans on undocumented executive assertions that they presented a security risk in World War II.[6] In 2004, this was a badge the Court would not wear.

II. How Far Did the Court Actually Go in the Guantanamo Case?

The Guantanamo inmates' challenge in *Rasul v. Bush*[7] came in the form of petitions for habeas corpus brought by relatives of natives of friendly countries—England, Australia, and Kuwait. The petitions claimed the detainees were innocent civilians captured abroad during the Afghanistan war by mistake who had never engaged in combat. This choice of plaintiffs had the advantage of giving a sympathetic international "feel" to the case. Indeed, the friendly status of their countries of origin was cited by the 6–3 majority as one of several factors that distinguished it from the *Eisentrager* precedent, which involved enemy alien members of the German army already convicted of war crimes by a military tribunal. Ironically, however, the non–enemy country's identity of the Guantanamo detainees could raise a question whether the vast bulk of Guantanamo detainees who are natives of Afghanistan, our avowed enemy at the time, are entitled to the relief provided in its ruling. Because the Court never suggests

6. *Korematsu v. United States*, 319 U.S. 432 (1943).
7. *Rasul v. Bush*, 124 S. Ct. 2686 (2004).

at any point in its reasoning that these detainees are not so entitled—
nor has the Pentagon acted on any such distinction since the decision—it is safe to presume that all Guantanamo inmates have equal
access to the writ, though obviously a native of our wartime enemy
may have greater difficulty proving his innocent status if captured on
or near the battlefield.

In granting access to the habeas corpus writ for the petitioner
detainees, the 6–3 fragmented Court in *Rasul* wrote a quite technical
opinion, heavily laden with arcane history of the writ and legal peculiarities of its varied applications. The Court saved its rousing rhetoric
for the *Hamdi* case and some members for their dissent in *Padilla*—
both cases dealing with American citizens.[8] At several junctures, the
Rasul plurality opinion, authored by Justice Stevens (joined by
Justices O'Connor, Souter, Ginsburg, and Breyer; Justice Kennedy

8. *Rumsfeld v. Padilla,* 124 S. Ct. 2711 (2004). *Padilla* was the last of the trilogy
of enemy combatant cases and involved an American citizen apprehended at O'Hare
Airport and detained first as a material witness and later turned over to the military
as an enemy combatant designated by presidential decree. A ruling on the merits
was detoured temporarily by a 5–4 decision dismissing his petition for habeas corpus
because his counsel did not file it in the district to which he had been transferred
as a prisoner but rather the one in which he was originally held. The substantive
holding in *Hamdi,* however, seems eminently applicable to his case, and his counsel
won a writ for his release in the district mandated by the Court, now on appeal.
Even so, Justice Stevens, writing for himself and Justices Souter, Ginsburg, and
Breyer, thought this an "exceptional case" where "slavish application" to a "bright
line rule" was uncalled for, since Padilla's counsel had not been given fair notice of
his impending transfer to South Carolina from New York, where she filed the writ.
In addition, Justice Stevens found the case "singular" because "th[e]se decisions have
created a unique and unprecedented threat to the freedom of every American citizen." The government had conceded in the lower court that the principal purpose
for Padilla's detention was "to find out everything he knows," provoking this exco-
riating reaction from Justice Stevens:

At stake in this case is nothing less than the essence of a free society.
Even more important than the method of selecting the people's rulers
and their successors is the character of the constraints imposed on the
Executive by the rule of law. Unconstrained Executive detention for the
purpose of investigating or preventing subversive activities is the hall-
mark of the Star Chamber.

concurred in the judgment only), stressed how "narrow but important" was the question before the Court, that question being strictly limited to whether the writ was available for "judicial review of the legality of Executive detention of aliens in a territory over which the United States exercises plenary and exclusive jurisdiction, but not 'ultimate sovereignty.'" In answering that question affirmatively, the Court first distinguished *Eisentrager* on several grounds, including the enemy alien status of the World War II prisoners and their prior convictions by a U.S. military tribunal for war crimes contrasted with the friendly nation origins of these prisoners and their as yet untried claims of total innocence. However, these differences, the Court emphasized, went only to the detainees' constitutional right to habeas, and their ultimate rights to habeas were based on the habeas statute, 28 U.S.C. § 2241, which had been reinterpreted since *Eisentrager* to allow the writ for U.S. captives held abroad, whether foreigners or U.S. citizens. It then said that the naval base was "within the territorial jurisdiction" of the United States due to the country's "complete jurisdiction and control" over anyone and everything that went on inside it. The Cuban government's retention of some ephemeral "ultimate sovereignty" should the United States choose not to exercise its perennial option to renew the ninety-nine-year lease had no practical or legal effect in this context. Thus, the normal presumption against extraterritorial application of domestic law did not apply. Most critically, the basic habeas corpus statute required only that the Court have jurisdiction over the custodian, not the prisoner—a proposition to which there was no disagreement among the parties here, because the writ was filed in the District of Columbia where the defendants (the president and the secretary of defense) resided. It could not be asserted, the Court concluded, that an American citizen residing or working on the Guantanamo base could not obtain the writ, and the habeas statute itself made no distinction between citizens and aliens in its geographical scope. The final word: These detainees had access to the writ.

But what precisely did the Court decide in *Rasul*, and what exactly does the executive branch have to do to meet it? How much leeway does it leave the executive in setting an altered detention regime for foreign prisoners captured on or near or even far away from the battlefield and not accorded prisoner of war (POW) status? If habeas lies, in which federal court does it lie? As to the last question, for now, it appears to lie in the D.C. Circuit, where the original cases were filed and the secretary of defense resides (the Court has already remanded the Ninth Circuit case for a ruling on whether the writ filed there should be dismissed for lack of jurisdiction). But what happens if the prisoners are moved, as the media report is under consideration, to mainland U.S. bases? Will the *Padilla* case, which dismissed the writ because it was not brought in the district where the prisoner was held and where his immediate warden (not Secretary Rumsfeld) resided, then govern? Probably. And does habeas really lie for every Guantanamo prisoner or, as the majority's closing line might suggest, only for those claiming innocence "of any wrongdoing"— that is, would someone who admitted or confessed under interrogation to participating in combat or in terrorist activity against the United States or even of being affiliated in some manner with al Qaeda be automatically denied the right to habeas? The scope of the Court's ruling on this all-important question was laconic:

> Whether and what further proceedings may become necessary after respondents make their response to the merits of petitioners' claims are matters that we need not address now. Only at stake was the federal court's jurisdiction to determine the legality of the Executive's potentially indefinite detention of individuals who claim to be wholly innocent of wrongdoing.

Over but hardly out. The Court had gotten its feet wet, but only a little.

This limited interpretation of the Court's own ruling inevitably elicits a broader question of what the scope of the habeas hearing can include. Will the detainee be limited to arguing only that he was not an enemy fighter or terrorist? Or can he also argue that he had rights under customary international law or the Geneva Conventions to fight for the Taliban and thus merited at least POW status? If not captured on or near the battlefield, can he maintain that the government had no grounds under international law on which to justify his summary detention without charges or trial on mere allegations that he had "affiliations," "connections with," gave "support to," or "harbored" terrorists plotting against the United States (many detainees were in fact apprehended far from the battlefield, in Bosnia, Yemen, Saudi Arabia, etc.)? Are the criteria laid down in the Court's companion *Hamdi* decision (discussed subsequently) for determining whether a foreign-born detainee is an enemy combatant different from those applicable to an American-born one, like Hamdi himself? Can the foreign-born prisoner's detention outlast the end of a war in which he fought until it is determined he is no longer a risk to the United States if returned to his home? (Reportedly, several Guantanamo inmates released voluntarily by the United States to their home countries have joined the terrorist ranks.) Finally, can an inmate argue in his habeas hearing that abusive treatment he received at Guantanamo violates the tenets of international humanitarian law (the law of war) even if he is validly determined to be an enemy combatant? Already, a new wave of cases (68 in the D.C. Circuit alone) have been filed involving virtually all of these questions and have begun their slow trek to the Supreme Court.[9] This second round will, if anything, require more difficult balancing and more nuanced constitutional interpretation than the first. All things considered, it

9. One district judge has ruled that there is "no viable legal theory" to support the release of seven of the detainees captured in Bosnia and Pakistan. The ruling said that the current military reviews provide process roughly equivalent to Article 5 of the Geneva Convention. Charles Lane and John Mintz, *Detainees Lose Bid for Release*, WASH. POST, Jan 20, 2005, at A3. Another judge, however, has ruled in the detainees' favor. Both cases are currently under appeal.

seems prudent of the Court to have left these decisions to be sorted out in the lower judicial echelons. There appears to be no danger they will not be pursued.

Within days of the *Rasul* decision, the Pentagon announced it would inform all detainees of their right to file habeas and would begin its own hearings to decide who is or is not an enemy combatant and who is no longer a risk and can be sent home. These military hearings permit the prisoner to appear before a three-person military panel and have a military-appointed personal advocate, but not his own lawyer.[10] However, the prisoner is not allowed to see secret evidence upon which his detention may be based. Although the government originally did not plan to let lawyers into the facility to aid prisoners, even those who don't speak English, in filing their writs, a federal judge has now required that the original *Rasul* petitioners be allowed speedy access to their lawyers and that their conversations be unmonitored.[11] The Pentagon has also sent a number of prisoners back to their home countries on its own. Still, it is not unlikely that the newly erected multimillion-dollar holding facility at Guantanamo will continue to be used for its intended purpose indefinitely.[12]

In addition, other extraordinarily important questions not yet the subject of litigation are in the wings. Justice Scalia, dissenting in

10. As of mid-December, more than 500 of the 550 hearings had been completed and only two released, although final rulings were pending in others. Associated Press, *Guantanamo Review to Free Second Man*, WASH. POST, Dec. 21, 2004, at A22.

11. Carol D. Leonnig, *U.S. Loses Ruling on Monitoring of Detainees*, WASH. POST, Oct. 21, 2004, at A4.

12. See White, supra note 9 (annual review instituted to see if detainees can be released; 150 were released before review begun); Don Van Natta Jr. and Tim Golden, *Officials Detail a Detainee Deal by 3 Countries*, N.Y. TIMES, July 31, 2004, at A1 and A8 (swap of British prisoners in Saudi Arabia for Saudis released from Guantanamo); Mintz, *Most at Guantanamo to Be Tried*, supra note 9 (deputy commander's view that most inmates "may pose little threat and are not providing much valuable intelligence" disputed by other officials; 146 released and 56 returned to home governments so far); Dana Priest, *Long-Term Plan Sought for Terror Suspects*, WASH. POST, Jan. 2, 2005, at A1 (administration preparing long-range plans for indefinite imprisoning of suspected terrorists it does not plan to bring to trial).

Rasul, highlighted one; Justice Thomas, dissenting in *Hamdi,* alluded to another. Justice Scalia said the majority opinion "boldly extends the scope of the habeas statute to the four corners of the earth," anywhere a U.S. custodian of foreign prisoners can be reached, and in so doing "springs a trap on the Executive," which had relied on settled law to the effect that habeas must be brought within a federal judicial district where the prisoner is being held. No such district in Guantanamo exists; according to Scalia, "that should be the end of the case." The consequences of the extension, Scalia warned, will be "breathtaking"; multitudes of aliens previously held abroad after capture in combat can now file habeas petitions in the United States, with the attendant problems of transporting them, as well as witnesses for both prosecution and defense, to the United States and taking military officers away from their field duties to testify. All this will, he said, aid and comfort the enemy. Our courts will be deluged.[13] And whether his parade of horribles is hyperbolic, Justice Scalia does make a point that is not immediately refutable: If the U.S. naval base at Guantanamo is U.S. territory because of the total U.S. control over what happens on it, other bases set up in occupied or even liberated Afghanistan and Iraq or other parts of the world may also be considered U.S. territory. It is a fact that we currently have hundreds of prisoners incarcerated in foreign-based facilities, with no access to judicial review as to the grounds for their apprehension or the duration or conditions of their confinement.[14] Likewise, Justice Thomas

13. Justice Scalia suggested a special district court could be established by Congress on Guantanamo to hear the cases.

14. See Douglas Jehl and Kate Zernike, *Scant Evidence Cited in Long Detention of Iraqis,* N.Y. TIMES, May 29, 2003, at A1 and A10 (hundreds of Iraqi prisoners held in Abu Ghraib for prolonged period despite lack of evidence of security threat, Army report says; 6,500 Iraqi detainees held in Iraq); *CIA's Prisoners* (ed.), WASH. POST, July 15, 2004, at A20 (al Qaeda senior leaders held incommunicado in undisclosed locations, not accessible to Red Cross); Bradley Graham and Josh White, *General Cites Hidden Detainees,* WASH. POST, Sept. 10, 2004, at A24 (up to 100 detainees concealed in military facilities abroad).

asks in the *Hamdi* ruling, if notice and some kind of hearing is necessary to detain a battlefield captive for any prolonged length of time, is it not also required when U.S. paramilitary operations "take out" suspected terrorists all around the world?

Circumstances often compel courts to be pragmatic, in the eyes of doctrinal purists, even arbitrary. The logic of a court's rationale may not have to be taken to its limit because that limit is totally impractical or potentially undesirable for nonlegal reasons. Constitutionally, there may also be separation-of-powers concerns that call for drawing lines in the sand. Thus, the Court limited its certiorari to the question of Guantanamo inmates and several times in the opinion stressed that was all it was deciding. Having made its decision in their favor, however, the Court certainly must have recognized that a second wave of cases would inevitably follow, claiming other U.S. bases or facilities in which prisoners are held abroad also meet the "complete jurisdiction and control" test that qualified Guantanamo as a U.S. territory. And although it is at least arguable that citizens of some of the countries in which U.S. authorities detain combatants and civilians may have more potential access to local courts or that the terms of the U.S. leases may be more temporary or conditional, human rights advocates (nor probably the Supreme Court as well) will hardly be content with a jurisprudence of individual rights based on property law.

It may also be argued that the Guantanamo situation is sui generis as a legitimate application or modest extension of international law concepts that the United States has already embraced. If, for instance, the United States had recognized as applicable, at least to Taliban fighters, the Third Geneva Convention on Treatment of Prisoners and the POW protocol set out therein and if the convention's Article 5 hearings had been held to sort out the totally innocent from the illegal combatants (something the Pentagon says it is now doing but too late to avoid the Court's habeas ruling), then these measures might have inclined the Court to stop at a few sentences in a per curiam opinion or even a denial of certiorari, leaving things as they were. That, of course, did not happen, and it was necessary for the Court to venture in deeper because the executive had refused to take any steps to provide process for the detainees akin to that laid down by international law for wars between state belligerents. Thus, the outcome might be different (or at least the argument can be made) in situations where no such close relationship to the Geneva-type conflict exists, as in the case of terrorists picked up abroad who are operating outside a traditional war setting. *Eisentrager* was not explicitly overruled by *Rasul* and could maintain legitimacy in these other factual settings. The geographic and situational scope of *Rasul* was left to a case-by-case determination in the future; it is plain that the principles by which these determinations will be made are still murky, but it is difficult to see how it could be otherwise.

The question also remains after *Rasul* whether an alien can be detained by U.S. authorities solely for interrogation or intelligence gathering, even though a citizen, under the *Hamdi* opinion (discussed subsequently), may not. Early on, Pentagon spokespersons said Guantanamo was chosen because they "wanted to put captives out of commission and find out what they knew."[15] The government's affidavits throughout the court proceedings in both *Hamdi* and *Padilla* posited the need to keep prisoners away from counsel, friends, and family in order to create a dependence on their interrogators that would lead to intelligence revelations. The plurality in *Hamdi*, however, ruled out interrogation as a reason to detain a U.S. citizen, and Justice Stevens, dissenting in *Padilla*, expounded:

> Executive detention of subversive citizens, like detention of enemy soldiers to keep them off the battlefield, may sometimes be justified to prevent persons from launching or becoming missiles of destruction. It may not, however, be justified by the naked

15. Scott Higham, Joe Stephens, and Margot Williams, *Guantanamo—A Holding Cell in War on Terrorism*, WASH. POST, May 2, 2004, at A1 and A15.

interest in using unlawful procedures to extract information. Incommunicado detention for months on end is such a procedure.

Yet, the value of detainees as a source of information remains high in the view of a substantial part of the intelligence community, and its dilution by legal restraints is likely to be vigorously opposed or circumscribed. The justices are worldly men and women and not oblivious to such concerns. The *Rasul* case does not touch the problem of whether detainees from foreign countries can be kept for intelligence purposes even if U.S. citizens can't. It seems plain after *Rasul* and *Hamdi* that Congress should tackle the problem directly and openly rather than asking the Court to determine it on the basis of old rules established for old problems in old kinds of war.

At this point, though, it seems safe to predict that the laws of war, though not specifically alluded to in the *Rasul* opinion, will ensure that battlefield detainees can be kept in temporary holding places in nearby safe places for reasonable periods of time until their status can be sorted out. During that time, they can also be questioned. But longer-term non-POWs removed far from the theater of combat, especially those kept only for intelligence reasons, are more susceptible to falling into the *Rasul* rationale.

The almost universal repulsion to the graphically displayed episodes of Iraqi prisoners at the U.S.-controlled Abu Ghraib prison being abused, and even dying, during interrogations cannot be discounted in any prediction of what the Court will do. The Court may well be inclined not to keep a hands-off policy on a problem of that size or gravity. The United States is, after all, a signer of the Convention Against Torture, which provides a cause of action for torture victims, including aliens, wherever detained. Thus, the *Rasul* Court's express finding that Guantanamo inmates may bring suit under the Alien Tort Claims Act is already being used in new lawsuits alleging that torture was in fact employed during interrogations there. Prisoners in other U.S. facilities around the world, perhaps even subjects of CIA or other counter-terrorism operations, can be expected to fol-low suit.[16]

An even trickier question is the one suggested by Justice Tho-mas. The *Rasul* ruling assumes prisoners, like the plaintiffs, were apprehended at or near the battlefield, though many in Guantanamo actually were captured as suspected terrorists elsewhere. The CIA, pursuant to explicit presidential findings disclosed to congressional leaders, engages in worldwide covert operations that result in appre-hension of noncombatants and their extended detention for interro-gation (or worse). Are these situations likely candidates for a *Rasul*-like ruling? The Geneva Conventions have no apparent application to such cases, unless perhaps the subjects are residents of occupied countries like Iraq.[17] The treatment of these subjects is accordingly a matter of domestic law, either of our own country or of the country where they are being held. But the Court's habeas-based reasoning could very well be analogized to their situation, in which case the repercussions on our antiterrorism efforts might be extreme indeed. Conversely, a court might plausibly hold that habeas in that setting would interfere with the executive's preeminent duty to protect the nation. Justice Thomas, in his *Hamdi* dissent, explicitly recognized the validity of intelligence gathering as a valid interest of the govern-ment that must be given due consideration in striking the due process balance between individual liberty and national security.

Finally, the *Rasul* opinion by itself gives no clue as to what

16. See Neil A. Lewis, *Fresh Details Emerge on Harsh Methods at Guantanamo*, N.Y. TIMES, Jan 1, 2005, at A11 (government-released memoranda in American Civil Liberties lawsuit revealing harsh interrogation practices in Guantanamo); Barton Gellman and R. Jeffrey Smith, *Report to Defense Alleged Abuse by Prison Interroga-tion Teams*, WASH. POST, Dec. 8, 2004, at A1 (internal Defense report cited reports of beatings of detainees by special military task force in Iraq); Neil A. Lewis, *U.S. Court Asserts Authority Over American in Saudi Jail*, N.Y. TIMES, Dec. 17, 2004, at A13 (District judge finds jurisdiction over suit by American jailed in Saudi Arabia as a terrorism suspect who alleges he is detained at behest of American officials).

17. See Dana Priest, *Memo Lets CIA Take Detainees Out of Iraq*, WASH. POST, Oct. 24, 2004, at A1.

procedures are due in any habeas process. By contrast, the *Hamdi* opinion sets out in reasonable detail those processes due an American citizen imprisoned as an enemy combatant. But Hamdi's rights derive largely from his constitutional rights as a citizen, which may well be greater than those accorded an alien; even the president's authority to define who is an enemy combatant may be wider in the case of a foreign-born person than of a citizen. Following the Court's *Rasul* decision, a Bush administration supporter remarked dourly, "If I were a detainee, I wouldn't be breaking out the champagne"; a prominent practitioner before the Court agreed, comparing the Court with someone "test driving a number of different principles without actually forking over a down payment."[18]

District court judges are independent, often stubborn, and even ornery when it comes to standing passively and watching their regular processes shortcut. Until the Supreme Court rules that foreign detainees are not entitled to the same procedural rights as citizens, the trial courts are likely to require appointed counsel, when appropriate, and the necessary degree of discovery required to sort out factual questions. In the words of the *Washington Post*, "Having blundered its way into federal court oversight of detentions at the camp, the government will now have to figure out how to meaningfully facilitate judicial review."[19] But it is not just the government that has been figuring out what to do; the federal judiciary and eventually the Supreme Court, which, in my view, correctly entered the fray, will inevitably become the final arbiter on this series of knotty questions — that is, unless Congress acts decisively and constitutionally in the near future.

18. Charles Lane, *Finality Seems to Elude High Court's Grasp*, WASH. POST, July 4, 2004, at A12.

19. See "Belated Reform," *supra* note 2. But see Carol D. Leonnig, *U.S. Defends Detentions*, WASH. POST, Oct. 5, 2004, at A10 (U.S. defending suits by 60 Guantanamo prisoners says it need not explain reasons for detention or apprehension far from battlefield under Commander-in-Chief power "to prevent captured individuals from serving the enemy").

III. What Did *Hamdi* Decide and
How Does It Interact with *Rasul?*

The second enemy combatant case, *Hamdi v. Rumsfeld*, involved an American citizen, captured by the Northern Alliance somewhere in Afghanistan and handed over to the American forces. The president designated Hamdi an enemy combatant, and Hamdi was subsequently incarcerated in a South Carolina military brig, held incommunicado with no access to family or counsel for more than two years. His father, as best friend, brought habeas; the government proffered to the court a nine-paragraph affidavit from a midlevel Pentagon officer and based on hearsay asserting Hamdi was fighting for the Taliban in an Afghanistan combat zone. The Fourth Circuit found the affidavit sufficient to support the president's designation and refused Hamdi access to counsel or to the court to refute the assertions.

The Supreme Court, seemingly much more comfortable in expressing varying emotions of outrage, commitment to old-line values, and skepticism about the executive's "Trust Us" contentions in a case involving an American citizen than in one involving an alien, came down on the side of Hamdi in four separate opinions with three different rationales, none commanding a majority but together involving eight of the nine justices (Justice Thomas was the holdout). The issue was framed by Justice O'Connor in her four-person plurality opinion. The Court was called upon, she said, to decide "the legality of the Government's detention of a United States citizen on United States soil as an enemy combatant and . . . the process that is constitutionally owed to one who seeks to challenge his classification as such." So far as we know, only three U.S. citizens have been so designated, compared with the hundreds of aliens imprisoned in Guantanamo. But the Court was on firmer ground doctrinally when it addressed the constitutional rights of U.S. citizens, and its discussion of remedies was far more detailed than the simple acknowledg-

ment of habeas jurisdiction in *Rasul*. Indeed, it was detailed enough
to invoke the "Mr. Fix-it Mentality" jibe of Justice Scalia, who
(together with Justice Stevens) nonetheless surprisingly would have
given Hamdi even greater relief than did the majority.

Justice O'Connor (writing for herself, Chief Justice Rehnquist,
and Justices Kennedy and Breyer) made several key rulings. The most
controversial, for some civil libertarians, was that the president had
authority under the Authorization of the Use of Military Force
(AUMF) resolution, passed by Congress in the wake of 9/11, to detain
anyone alleged, as Hamdi was, to be "part of or supporting forces
hostile to the United States or coalition partners in Afghanistan and
who engaged in an armed conflict against the United States there."
She made abundantly clear, however, that this was the exclusive definition of an "enemy combatant" that the opinion would deal with
(despite recognition that the government had attached the label to a
much broader array of prisoners, including an American seized on
American soil suspected of plotting terrorism with al Qaeda and suspected confederates of al Qaeda seized far from any battlefield and
held at Guantanamo and elsewhere around the world). However, this
limited definition of an enemy combatant, O'Connor continued,
allowed the detention of such persons to conform to the laws of war.
Adherence to the laws of war, in turn, meant that their detention was
included within the "necessary and appropriate force" that the AUMF
resolution authorized to be used on al Qaeda–affiliated persons and
those who harbored them—in this case, the Taliban. The resolution,
so interpreted, trumped an earlier U.S. statute passed in 1971, 18
U.S.C. § 4001, proscribing the detention of any U.S. citizen except
pursuant to an act of Congress. (Interestingly, Justices Stevens, Scalia,
Souter, and Ginsburg, in separate opinions, specifically disagreed
with this ruling on the nonapplicability of 18 U.S.C. § 4001's bar to
Hamdi, and Justice Breyer joined a dissent written by Justice Stevens
in *Padilla* to the same effect.) Thus, by relying on international customary law—here, the laws of war—as the basis for detention of non-

POW captives, the O'Connor opinion bypassed the government's argument that Article II of the Constitution gave the president, as commander-in-chief, virtually absolute power to designate someone as an enemy combatant without individual judicial review of any sort.

A power to detain, without charges or trial, battlefield combatants not qualifying for POW treatment under the laws of war is supported by many, but certainly not all, international law experts. There are a significant number who argue that any power to detain battlefield captives other than as POWs or for specific war crimes must come from domestic law and is not found in either the Geneva Conventions or customary international law. If they are right, the 1971 statute adopted to outlaw noncongressionally authorized citizen internment would apply, and Hamdi could not be held. Justice Souter's separate concurrence in the judgment (joined by Justice Ginsburg) found that the drafters of the 1971 statute did indeed mean it to apply robustly in wartime as well as in peacetime. It was especially needed in a separation-of-powers regime, he said, where "deciding . . . what is a reasonable degree of . . . liberty whether in peace or war is not well-entrusted to the Executive Branch . . . whose particular responsibility is to maintain security."

The authorization for "necessary and appropriate force" in the AUMF resolution was not a clear enough statement of congressional intent to repeal the prior 1971 ban on citizen detention. Justice Souter hedged a bit at the end, however, acknowledging that if the laws of war did allow detentions of battlefield combatants lasting for the duration of the war, then that might justify Hamdi's detention as consistent with the earlier statute. But because the United States itself was guilty of violating these same laws of war by not providing Hamdi any process for demonstrating his innocence, as was required by Article 5 of the Third Geneva Convention, which Justice Souter said the United States admitted applied to Taliban fighters, the United States could not seek haven in the laws of war to authorize the detention and overcome the 1971 law.

Justice O'Connor did not deal with this contention of Justice Souter and of many international law experts, that the Taliban was the official armed force of a state party to the Geneva Conventions and that Taliban fighters (apart from al Qaeda partisans) should have been recognized as POWs. That omission may be explained in part because the nature of Hamdi's activities in Afghanistan were in dispute (he claimed to be a total innocent); in any case, there was the government's counter that determining whether fighters for an enemy's regime are recognized as POWs under the Geneva Conventions is a quintessential political judgment of the executive, which the Court should not second-guess. On the other hand, there are many internationalists who would say POW recognition is a treaty obligation that a country must obey and that should be enforceable by its own domestic courts, as well as by international courts. The skirting of the issue by Justice O'Connor, however, weakens, to some degree, the logic of her complex rationale supporting the president's power to detain even the limited group of enemy combatants that came within her opinion's definition. Should the United States go to war again and pursue a like policy of refusing POW status to Geneva Convention Party soldiers, the question is sure to resurface. In Iraq, the United States formally recognized Iraqi army captives as POWs.

On the other hand, a positive byproduct of Justice O'Connor's reliance on the laws of war for support of Hamdi's detention is her statement that detention of enemy combatants is limited under the laws of war to the duration of the particular conflict in which the detainees participated. The specter of indefinite detention past the end of the immediate armed conflict, be it Afghanistan or Iraq or wherever, in the name of an endless worldwide war against terrorism or even against al Qaeda obviously disturbed the Court, which was relying on laws of war principles applicable to traditional wars—that reliance, it warned, could "unravel" in the case of a conflict entirely unlike past wars. In Hamdi's case, however, armed conflict still raged in Afghanistan. He could be detained while U.S. troops were still involved. But, O'Connor steadfastly maintained, detention under the laws of war is for the purposes of holding the detainees off the battlefield. "[C]ertainly," the opinion stated, "indefinite detention for the purposes of interrogation is not authorized" either by the laws of war or by the AUMF resolution. This limitation poses significant obstacles to the executive's earlier announced intentions to keep battlefield detainees incarcerated as long as the United States thinks they serve an intelligence purpose or pose a risk to our security.

In the end, although much is left open by the plurality opinion dealing with the definition of an enemy combatant, it should be recognized that much is decided as well. It does not decide whether the president, as commander-in-chief, has any such detention power on his own without congressional consent. It does not go beyond a definition of a detainable enemy combatant as one who took up arms against U.S. or allied forces on a specific battlefield (the plurality opinion leaves any expansion of this definition to district courts in future cases), and it appears to assume the duration of detention is restricted to the length of the defined conflict, rejecting any extended incarceration for the purpose of interrogation. It does not decide whether any of these limitations of definition, purpose, or duration apply to foreign-born enemy combatants, though logic and international human rights law suggest most of them should, and human rights activists will surely continue to push for their inclusion. It avoids all questions of whether and to what degree the Geneva Conventions apply to enemy combatants in the Afghanistan war (except as to the duration of detention). Importantly, it uses international law—the laws of war—as the linchpin of its rationale rejecting the applicability of a domestic statute that on its face appears to outlaw the detention.

The final step in Justice O'Connor's regimen for detention of citizen enemy combatants was to list the rudiments of due process that the citizen detainee must receive; this included, under the habeas statute, notice of the charges against him and the right to deny such charges and produce any material evidence in his defense (evidence under the habeas statute may be taken by deposition, interrogatories, or affidavit, as well as through live witnesses). More basically, she used a balancing of individual liberty and governmental interests, as set out in *Mathews v. Eldridge*,[20] a welfare benefits case, to define the core rights of a detainee to include notice of the factual basis for his classification as an enemy combatant and an opportunity to rebut those presumptions before a neutral decision maker. Significantly, in weighing the competing interests, she narrowly defined the government's "weighty and sensitive interests" as "assuring that those who have in fact fought with the enemy during a war do not return to battle against the United States" and eloquently described the individual's interest as "the most elemental of liberty interests—the interest in being free from physical detention by one's own government," an interest as strong in war as in peace, an interest not diminished even by an accusation of treason. "It is during our most challenging and uncertain moments that our Nation's commitment to due process is most severely tested." She did, however, entertain the possibility that the detainee's hearing might be "tailored" to offset the alleged burdens on field personnel performing essential military duties. The tailoring might include greater use of hearsay and a rebuttable presumption in favor of the government's evidence; even an "appropriately authorized and properly constituted military tribunal" might suffice. This last suggestion was an invitation the Pentagon seized promptly, instituting a military review process within days of the opinion's issuance, which the Pentagon said would supplement, not supplant, the habeas proceeding. According to the opinion, the hearing need not be held immediately on the battlefield; it could be held within a reasonable time when the decision is made to continue the detention.[21]

20. *Mathews v. Eldridge*, 434 U.S. 319 (1976).

21. Although Justices Souter and Ginsburg voted with the plurality to make a majority for the remand hearing, they disassociated themselves from the portion of

Hamdi, however, had been given no process at all. The government claimed in its affidavit that "undisputed" evidence showed he had been captured in a combat zone and that was sufficient. The Court rejected that argument: The circumstances of his capture were not undisputed at all—his father's affidavit said only that Hamdi resided in Afghanistan at the time of his seizure, and he was never allowed to answer the charges that he was fighting for the Taliban. And, even if undisputed, his seizure in a combat zone would not be proof that he was engaged in an armed conflict against the United States or its partners, which was the only definition of an enemy combatant acceptable in this case.

Addressing the broader separation of powers contention of the government (and Justice Thomas), Justice O'Connor further rejected the argument that the courts could review only the executive's broad detention scheme, not its application in individual cases. "Whatever power the United States Constitution envisions for the Executive in its exchanges with other nations or with enemy organizations in times of conflict, it most assuredly envisions a role for all three branches when individual liberties are at stake."

There is no doubt that what journalist Anthony Lewis called the president's "presumptuous omnipotence"[22] had been checked. The judiciary would be watching and, theoretically, ready to move on the wartime detention process at critical stages. It had established its outpost. Hearings would not, as the doomsayers predicted, be required on the battlefield. A hybrid procedure short of the usual full court habeas hearing in every case might be crafted that would satisfy due

---

the plurality that dealt with any "tailoring" of the detention hearing involving greater use of hearsay or a rebuttable presumption in favor of government evidence. And they did not agree that a military-type hearing could obviate the need for a regular habeas corpus proceeding. They could, however, envision government power to detain "in a moment of genuine emergency, when the Government must act with no time for deliberation . . . if there is reason to fear that [the citizen] is an imminent threat to the safety of the Nation and its people."

22. Anthony Lewis, *The Court v. Bush,*" N.Y. TIMES, June 29, 2004, at A27.

process and not unduly burden military personnel or distract them from battlefield duties, though the acceptance of a procedure that put the burden of disproving the government's evidence on the petitioners gave civil libertarians great pause.[23] (This may have been one place where less detail on possible accommodations to the basic habeas right might have been more prudent.) And the lower courts would have to take the initiative in deciding how much further the concept of an enemy combatant could be extended for summary detention purposes.

Perplexing, however, is the extent to which the rationale and rights set out in the *Hamdi* plurality apply to noncitizens, who do not necessarily enjoy all the constitutional rights of U.S. citizens. Does their liberty interest, for instance, rank lower in the *Mathews v. Eldridge* balance? Ironically, many come from countries where no liberty interest at all in these circumstances would be recognized. If the *Hamdi* safeguards do not apply to citizen and noncitizen detainees alike, but foreigners (at least the Guantanamo inmates) do have access to habeas, exactly which rights will *Hamdi* give noncitizens? Aliens in habeas actions have not traditionally received a lesser degree of procedural protections, but the courts have never before been faced with hundreds, or even thousands, of such detainees, many allegedly intent upon injuring our own citizens as soon as they are released, and some having no place to which they can be safely returned. The government could presumably try the most dangerous for war crimes or even under our domestic criminal laws (it already has a half dozen slated for military tribunals), but even with controversially restricted

---

23. It's not clear whether the military tribunal to which Justice O'Connor referred would require counsel. The Army Regulations and Article 5 of the Third Geneva Convention do not. Neither do the newly initiated Pentagon status hearings for Guantanamo inmates. Hamdi, however, was specifically accorded counsel on remand to assist him in his habeas hearing. Hamdi has since been released and sent back to Saudi Arabia under certain restrictions on his freedom to travel or concert with terrorist groups. See Jerry Markham, *Hamdi Returned to Saudi Arabia*, WASH. POST, Oct. 12, 2004, at A2.

defense rights, the military trials are proving extremely slow to mount.[24] A district court ruling, currently on appeal, has stayed all military tribunal proceedings on the ground that the detainees were denied their Geneva Convention rights to a hearing on whether they merited POW status or were innocent of any engagement in combat. If they were POWs, they could be tried only by court-martial under the convention.[25]

As to civilian courts, alleged obstructionist tactics and the due process problem of nondisclosable evidence and unavailable witnesses present real problems to their extensive use, as the ongoing *Moussaoui* trial indicates too well.[26] And the open question, discussed earlier, of what the foreign detainee can claim in a habeas hearing—for example, international law violations or torture contentions—further conflates the issue. Both the *Rasul* decision and the *Hamdi* plurality opinion seem to focus exclusively on the situation of a detainee protesting his complete innocence of any involvement in an armed conflict. More nuanced challenges to the legality of detention on other grounds may well require more guidance from the Court. But the variety of scenarios in which these challenges will rise would have made detailed protocols not only impossible but probably counterproductive. The Court signaled the path and a few markers—that is all it could or likely should have done.

24. Neil A. Lewis, *U.S. Terrorism Tribunal Set to Begin Work*, N.Y. TIMES, Aug. 22, 2004, at A17 (four detainees appear in court after three years, defense lawyers complain of inadequate translation help, anonymous witnesses, loose evidence rules, and no appeal to civilian authorities); Scott Higham, *Trials Set to Begin for Four at Guantanamo*, WASH. POST, Aug. 23, 2004, at A1 and A7 (conversations between defendants and lawyers can be monitored; exculpatory evidence can be kept secret; defense lawyers and human rights activists label proceedings "fundamentally unfair"); Neil A. Lewis, *Guantanamo Tribunal Process in Turmoil*, N.Y. TIMES, Sept. 26, 2004, at A20 (officials acknowledge the process is in turmoil).

25. Carol D. Leonnig and John Mintz, *Judge Says Detainees' Trials Are Unlawful*, WASH. POST, Nov. 9, 2004, at A1.

26. *The Tribunals Begin*, WASH. POST, Aug. 29, 2004, at B6.

IV. The *Hamdi* Dissent

Who would have suspected that the most civil liberties–oriented opinion in *Hamdi* would be authored by Justice Scalia in an odd-couple dissent with Justice Stevens? Justice Scalia's construct is clean and straightforward—the U.S. Constitution prescribes the procedural and definitional requirements for treason, and U.S. laws do the same for other crimes against national security. Also, the Constitution's Suspension Clause allows Congress to suspend the writ of habeas corpus temporarily in dire national emergencies. Any detention of a citizen can and must be handled within that framework. The congressional resolution on which the plurality relies to authorize these detentions does not and could not constitutionally legislate a third option. The history of the Great Writ, described in extraordinary detail in Justice Scalia's opinion, demonstrates that its principle raison d'être was to ensure due process before the executive can deprive a citizen of liberty under any circumstances. Thus, there could not be "a different special procedure for imprisonment of a citizen accused of wrongdoing by aiding the enemy in wartime." The laws of war might permit detention of enemy aliens for the duration but the tradition for American citizens is altogether different. American terrorists and traitors can be subjected to established criminal processes, and when those processes prove totally impracticable, the writ can be, and has on occasion, been suspended.

Precedents from the War of 1812 confirmed the absence of military authority to indefinitely imprison citizens in wartime outside of normal criminal procedures. *Ex parte Milligan*, in the Civil War, rejected the "usages of war" as a justification for putting a citizen of a nonseceding state before a military tribunal for sabotage while the civilian courts in his own locale were open and operating.[27] *Ex parte Quirin*, which allowed an American citizen to be tried by a military

---

27. *Ex parte Milligan*, 71 U.S. 2 (1866).

tribunal, is dismissed as "not this Court's finest hour."[28] However, it involved admitted German army saboteurs stealing into the United States during wartime, not citizens captured abroad who disputed any military involvement against the United States.

Justice Scalia, like Justice Souter, did not think the AUMF resolution specific enough to repeal the earlier ban against detention of citizens except pursuant to an act of Congress, and while the laws of war might authorize detention of foreigners as enemy combatants, it could never supersede constitutional requirements for detaining citizens. Justice Scalia, however, is careful to admit the "relatively narrow compass" of his profound ruling—it applies only to citizens detained within the territorial jurisdiction of a federal court. In sum, the writ is available—until suspended—only for citizens detained where a federal court operates (it is not clear whether Scalia thinks the military could transfer or keep U.S. citizens outside U.S. territory to avoid that requirement). Within these geographical limits, however, habeas would inevitably attain for them the full panoply of criminal trial rights, notice, discovery, counsel, civilian judge, even jury, and, in treason cases, the two witnesses to an overt act rule. Justice Scalia's decision sounds generous, and it is—to a degree—but it applies only to two cases so far and might even be avoidable by military canniness in locating prisoners outside federal judicial districts. We know that Justice Scalia would not recognize any jurisdiction over the Guantanamo inmates, and he suggests Congress might legislate a separate procedure for intelligence gathering, presumably from either foreigners or Americans. Within its narrow boundaries, Justice Scalia's rationale is liberal but it leaves the vast bulk of U.S.-held detainees outside its charmed circle.[29]

28. *Ex parte Quirin*, 63 S. Ct. 2 (1942).
29. Justice Thomas is odd man out. Not "Mr. Fix-it" surely, rather Mr. "Nothing is wrong—Just trust the executive." According to Justice Thomas, the detention of Americans as enemy combatants falls squarely within the president's war powers, courts have no competence or expertise to second-guess him. Although the Court

v. Conclusion—What to Make of It All?

Like its same-term *Blakeley* decision on sentencing, the Supreme
Court's entry into the arena of the war on terrorism is destined to
create immediate demands for more elucidation, more explanation,
and more intervention.[30] In the end, it is hard to give credence to
Justice Scalia's criticism that the Court had gone too far in laying
down protocols for executive treatment of wartime detainees. In some
ways, however, it may not have gone far enough, considering the
splintered rationales of the *Rasul* and *Hamdi* cases; to go much further might well have brought fragile coalitions down altogether. The
Court has ruled definitively on one aspect of the war—U.S. and foreign detainees housed in Guantanamo who are accused of being
enemy combatants fighting American forces in armed combat must
be allowed access to the ancient writ of habeas corpus if they claim
to be innocent bystanders, not combatants. In such a proceeding, U.S.
citizens must be accorded certain basic rights to notice and to defend
on the facts. Much more than that, we do not know. But for launching the quest, the Court deserves praise.

Some big questions remain unanswered. Does habeas lie for
foreign detainees housed elsewhere than at Guantanamo? Does it lie

---

has the right to look at Hamdi's case, it should do so only with "the strongest presumptions for the Government." It should look at whether the president had general
authority to detain enemy combatants, not how he exercised it in individual cases.
Nor should detention be limited to the duration of a particular conflict. In certain
contexts, "due process requires nothing more than a good-faith Executive determination"—the president has the power to make "virtually conclusive factual findings"
on who is an enemy combatant. Detention might be justified by the need for intelligence as well as preventing return to the battlefield. In Hamdi's case, he would not
grant counsel on remand or even notice of charges if it could destroy the intelligence-
gathering function of his detention.

30. *Blakeley v. Washington*, 124 S. Ct. 2531 (2004) (late in the 2003 term, Court
invalidated portions of state-sentencing guidelines regime, thereby throwing validity
of federal sentencing guidelines into grave doubt; within weeks, Court granted certiorari on the issue of their constitutionality with argument at beginning of October
2004 term and decision rendered in January 2005).

for claims of abuse or violations of international law apart from total innocence of being a combatant at all?[31] Do foreigners have the same rights at a habeas hearing as do American-born defendants?[32] How far can the designation of "enemy combatant" carry beyond the battlefield? Do targets of intelligence covert actions abroad have any rights comparable with enemy combatants?

The laws of war, as interpreted by the *Hamdi* plurality, were a key element of the decision, but they have no applicability beyond the battlefield or occupied territory and are not readily adaptable to the war on terrorism. The Geneva Conventions and progeny are badly in need of revision if they are to meet the realities of terrorist wars. But equally deficient is our own domestic law concerning who, under what conditions, with what procedures, and for how long battlefield captives can be held. The Supreme Court entered the arena because it had to; individual liberties guaranteed by our Constitution and laws to citizens (and, to some degree, to aliens) were in jeopardy.

31. President Bush's investigative commission cites 300 cases of alleged abuse at U.S.-controlled prisons abroad and urges that all prisoners be treated "in a way consistent with U.S. jurisprudence and military doctrine and with U.S. interpretation of the Geneva Conventions." Eric Schmidt, *Abuse Panel Says Rules on Inmates Need Overhaul*, N.Y. TIMES, Aug. 25, 2004, at A1. Army investigators similarly found that the CIA hid prisoners from international human rights groups. Josh White, *Abuse Report Widens Scope of Culpability*, WASH. POST, Aug. 26, 2004, at A1 and A16. See also R. Jeffrey Smith, *Agency Is Faulted on Practices in Iraq, Secrecy Amid Probe*, WASH. POST, Aug. 26, 2004, at A18 (Army report says that CIA's detentions and interrogation practices "led to a loss of accountability, abuse, reduced interagency cooperation and unhealthy mystique that . . . poisoned the atmosphere" in Abu Ghraib).

32. See United Nations Committee on Elimination of Racial Discrimination Resolution, 64th Session, Feb.–Mar. 2004 (state parties should "ensure that noncitizens detained or arrested in the fight against terrorism are properly protected by domestic law that complies with international human rights, refugee and humanitarian law"); American Bar Association House of Delegates Resolution, August 25, 2004 (condemning any use of torture or other cruel, inhumane, or degrading treatment or punishment upon persons within the custody or under the physical control of the U.S. government [including its contractors] and calling for an independent commission to prepare a full account of detentions and interrogations carried out by the United States).

The Court has momentarily finished the opening round, but the legal battles are still being waged. Before there are repetitions of the Afghanistan and Iraq wars, there needs to be a thoughtful debate on and legislative resolution of interrogation procedures and rights, detention limits on who and how long non-POWs can be held, and what, if any, rights adhere to targets of covert actions. It is long past time for Congress to become engaged—even though there are skeptics in the civil liberties community about what Congress may do. Congress is the branch of government directly responsible, along with the executive, to the citizenry for the reconciliation of wartime security and civil liberties, and Congress must fully accept this moment of responsibility.[33] Otherwise, there are bound to be much deeper interventions by the Court in this troubled area of the law. Once in the water, the Court may not be able to hug the shoreline much longer; instead, it will be carried irretrievably by the current out to the "boundless sea."

33. At the urging of the White House, the congressional conference committee on the Intelligence Reform Bill "scrapped a legislative measure that would have imposed new restrictions on the use of extreme interrogation measures by American intelligence officers." Douglas Jehl and David Johnston, *White House Fought New Curbs on Interrogations, Officials Say*, N.Y. TIMES, Jan. 13, 2005, at A1.

3. Enemy Combatants and the Problem of Judicial Competence

John Yoo

FROM THE INITIAL RETURNS, one might believe that the 2003–2004 October term of the Supreme Court dealt the Bush administration a defeat in the war on terrorism. *Rasul v. Bush* held that the federal courts—for the first time—will review the grounds for detaining alien enemy combatants held outside the United States.[1] In *Hamdi v. Rumsfeld*, the justices required that American citizens detained in the war have access to a lawyer and a fair hearing before a neutral judge.[2]

While the Court has unwisely injected itself into military matters, closer examination reveals that it has affirmed the administration's fundamental legal approach to the war on terrorism and left it with sufficient flexibility to effectively prevail in the future. Despite the pleas of legal and media elites, the Justices did not turn the clock back to September 10, 2001. Rather, the Court agreed that the United States is at war against the al Qaeda terrorist network and the Taliban militia that supports it. It agreed that Congress has authorized that war. The justices implicitly recognized that the United States may

1. *Rasul v. Bush*, 124 S. Ct. 2686 (2004).
2. *Hamdi v. Rumsfeld*, 124 S. Ct. 2633 (2004).

use all the tools of war to fight a new kind of enemy that has no territory, no population, and no desire to spare innocent civilian life. The days when terrorism was merely considered a law enforcement problem and our only forces were limited to the FBI, federal prosecutors, and the criminal justice system will not be returning.

Nonetheless, the Court also emphasized the importance of judicial review in assessing the cases of individual detainees captured in the war on terrorism. The Supreme Court made clear that it would no longer consider military decisions in wartime to be outside the competence of the federal courts. Instead, the judiciary would review the grounds for the detention of enemy combatants. Expansion of judicial review into military decisions represents an intrusion of the federal courts that is unprecedented on both formal and functional grounds. At the simplest, formal level, this expansion required the Court to effectively overrule a precedent decided at the end of World War II that was exactly on point.[3] At a broader, functional level, it will call on the judiciary to make factual and legal judgments in the midst of war, pressing the courts far beyond their normal areas of expertise and risking conflict with the other branches in the management of wartime measures.

This chapter discusses four issues. Part I explains why the events of September 11, 2001, demonstrate that terrorism has become a matter for war, rather than simply a crime. Part II argues that the Supreme Court's cases in *Hamdi* and *Rasul* accepted the judgment of the political branches on this important point; the government's authority to detain enemy combatants without charge followed. Part III discusses the Court's decision to require a certain level of due process for enemy combatants, both citizens and aliens, detained both within and outside the United States. Part IV questions whether the comparative institutional competencies of the judiciary make it a good choice to advance and to carry out national security and foreign policy.

3. *Johnson v. Eisentrager*, 339 U.S. 763 (1950).

I.

After the September 11 terrorist attacks, the United States went to war against the al Qaeda terrorist organization. On that day, al Qaeda operatives hijacked four commercial airliners and used them as guided missiles against the World Trade Towers in New York City and the Pentagon in the nation's capital. Resisting passengers brought down in Pennsylvania a fourth plane that appears to have been headed toward either the Capitol or the White House. The attacks caused about 3,000 deaths, disrupted air traffic and communications within the United States, and caused the economy billions of dollars in losses. Both the president and Congress agreed that the attacks marked the beginning of an armed conflict between the United States and the al Qaeda terrorist network.[4] Indeed, al Qaeda's September 11 attacks amounted to a classic decapitation strike designed to eliminate the political, military, and financial leadership of the country.

It may be useful at the outset to discuss the difference between al Qaeda and September 11, on the one hand, and the traditional wars that had characterized the nineteenth and twentieth centuries, on the other. While al Qaeda had conducted a series of attacks against the United States since the 1993 bombing of the World Trade Center, September 11 made salient the unconventional nature of both the war and the enemy. Al Qaeda is not a nation-state, nor is it an alter-ego supported by a nation state, which may distinguish it from the groups in the Vietnam War. As a nonstate actor, al Qaeda does not have a territory or population, nor does it seek to defend or acquire any specific territory. In this respect, it is unlike an indigenous rebel group that is fighting to replace an existing regime through an intrastate civil war.

Al Qaeda's operations are also unconventional and, as strategic

4. See President's Military Order "Detention, Treatment, and Trial of Certain Non-Citizens in the War Against Terrorism," 66 *Fed. Reg.* § 1(a), 57,833 (Nov. 13, 2001); *Authorization for Use of Military Force*, Pub. L. 107-40, 115 Stat. 224 (2001).

analysts like to say, asymmetric. Al Qaeda soldiers do not wear uniforms, and they do not operate in conventional units and force structures. Rather, their personnel, material, and leadership move through the open channels of the international economy and are organized in covert cells. Al Qaeda does not seek to close with and defeat the enemy's regular armed forces on the battlefield. Instead, it seeks to achieve its political aims by launching surprise attacks, primarily on civilian targets, through the use of unconventional weapons and tactics, such as concealed bombs placed on trains or using airplanes as guided missiles. Victory does not come from defeat of the enemy's forces and eventually a negotiated political settlement, rather it comes from demoralizing an enemy's society and coercing it to take desired action.

Another factor distinguishes the war against al Qaeda from previous wars. In previous modern American conflicts, hostilities were limited to a foreign battlefield, while the U.S. home front remained safe behind the distances of two oceans. In this conflict, however, the battlefield can occur anywhere, and there can be no strict division between the front and home. The September 11 attacks themselves, for example, were launched by foreign forces from within the United States, using American airliners, against targets wholly within the United States. While American territory has witnessed foreign attack in the past, most notably the attack on Pearl Harbor to launch World War II, September 11 constituted the first major attack on the continental United States, and on major American cities since the War of 1812.

Thus, like previous wars, an important dimension of the conflict with al Qaeda has occurred abroad, in which the U.S. armed forces and the intelligence agencies have played an offensive role aimed at destroying the terrorist network. In October 2001, the United States launched a military campaign in Afghanistan that within a few short weeks rooted out al Qaeda from its bases and removed from power

the Taliban militia that had harbored it.[5] The United States has conducted operations against al Qaeda terrorists in other parts of the
world, such as the Philippines, Yemen, and parts of Africa. It has
detained hundreds of al Qaeda and Taliban fighters as prisoners at
the naval base at Guantanamo Bay, Cuba. In March 2003, motivated
in part by Iraq's suspected links to terrorist groups in general and al
Qaeda specifically, the United States and its allies invaded Iraq and
removed Saddam Hussein from power.[6]

Unlike previous conflicts, however, the war against al Qaeda also
has a significant domestic dimension. The initial salvo was launched
by al Qaeda operatives against the United States from within the
United States. Al Qaeda shows no lessening in its efforts to pull off
another attack within the United States on the scale of September
11. The Justice Department has discovered al Qaeda cells in cities
such as Buffalo, New York, and Portland, Oregon; detained a resident
alien who had intended to destroy the Brooklyn Bridge; and inter-
cepted at least one American citizen in Chicago who had planned
to explode a radiological dispersal device, known as a "dirty bomb,"
in a major American city. After the attacks, the federal government
investigated and detained hundreds of illegal aliens within the United
States with possible links to the terrorists. Many were deported. Al
Qaeda agents taken into custody within the United States have been
designated as enemy combatants and are being detained without
criminal charge until the end of the conflict. Congress enacted legislation—the USA Patriot Act—to enhance the powers of the FBI

---

5. For my earlier discussions of the legal issues surrounding the Afghanistan
war, see Robert J. Delahunty and John Yoo, *The President's Constitutional Authority
to Conduct Military Operations Against Terrorist Organizations and the Nations That
Harbor or Support Them*, 25 HARV. J. L. & PUB. POLICY 487 (2002); John C. Yoo
and James C. Ho, *The Status of Terrorists*, 44 VA. J. INT'L L. 207 (2003).

6. Of course, the primary justifications for the war in Iraq were Hussein's continuing possession of a weapons of mass destruction (WMD) program and his flouting
of United Nations Security Council resolutions. See John Yoo, *International Law
and the War in Iraq*, 97 AM. J. INT'L L. 563 (2003).

and the intelligence community to defeat international terrorists within the United States,[7] and created a new Department of Homeland Security to consolidate twenty-two separate domestic agencies with responsibilities for domestic security.[8] After these legislative changes, the government engaged in an expanded surveillance effort to monitor the communications of terrorist targets under the Foreign Intelligence Surveillance Act.

It is this virtually unprecedented domestic dimension to the conflict that has led some to misunderstand the fundamental nature of the conflict with al Qaeda. They argue that terrorism is a tactic, not an enemy, and that this implies that the war on terrorism is a problem for the criminal law, as it was before September 11, 2001. The war on terrorism is no different conceptually from the war on drugs, the war on poverty, or the war on crime. These "wars" also have their own nonstate actors, such as drug cartels or organized crime groups. However, I believe September 11 is different in kind rather than degree. Perhaps the confusion arises from the political rhetoric of the "war on terrorism" and the actual conflict, which is between the United States and the al Qaeda terrorist organization and its affiliates. The United States is not at war with every group in the world that uses terrorist tactics. Furthermore, al Qaeda is different from a drug cartel or organized crime groups, and hence its defeat is more a matter for war than for crime.

Several reasons distinguish the war against the al Qaeda terrorist network from a large-scale criminal investigation or a broad and persistent social problem. First, al Qaeda represents a wholly foreign threat that emanates from outside the United States. This makes it different from homegrown terrorism, such as the bombing of the

7. *Uniting and Strengthening America by Providing Appropriate Tools Required to Intercept and Obstruct Terrorism* (USA PATRIOT) *Act*, Pub. L. No. 107-56, 115 Stat. 272 (2001).

8. Exec. Order No. 13,228, *Establishing the Office of Homeland Security and the Homeland Security Council*, 66 Fed. Reg. 51,812 (2001).

Oklahoma City federal building by Timothy McVeigh, which would be an appropriate subject for the criminal justice system. Second, al Qaeda is unlike a crime organization in that it seeks purely political ends, rather than acting out of a desire for gain or financial profit. Al Qaeda attacked the United States because it wants the United States to withdraw its military and political presence from the Middle East. It may seek financial gain to fund its terrorist operations to achieve that goal, but financial advancement is not its purpose. Third, al Qaeda has proven that it is capable of inflicting a level of violence on the United States that pushes its conduct beyond the realm of crime into that of war. While the location of the precise line between the violence of crime and that of war may not be certain, it seems clear that the September 11 attacks crossed that line, with their approximately 3,000 deaths and billions of dollars in damage.

II.

In *Hamdi*, the Supreme Court accepted the political branches' basic decision to characterize the September 11 attacks as war. In so doing, it rejected arguments that terrorism had to be understood solely as criminal activity, and it denied the notion that war could only occur against nations and not against nonstate actors as well.

During the fighting in Afghanistan, Yaser Hamdi was captured by Northern Alliance troops, a coalition of groups allied to the United States and opposed to the Taliban militia, and was handed over to the U.S. armed forces.[9] Hamdi was transferred to the naval station at Guantanamo Bay and then, upon discovery that he had been born in the United States, to a navy brig in South Carolina. He was not charged with a crime. Hamdi's father filed a writ of habeas corpus seeking his son's release, based on the claim that as an American citizen, Hamdi could not be held without criminal charges or access

---

9. These facts are taken from the Court's majority opinion. *Hamdi*, 124 S. Ct. 2633 (2004).

to a tribunal or counsel. He based his argument on 18 U.S.C. § 4001(a), which declares that "[n]o citizen shall be imprisoned or otherwise detained by the United States except pursuant to an Act of Congress." Although the government did not challenge Hamdi's right to seek habeas, it argued that he was detained lawfully as an enemy combatant under the laws of war. It refused to allow Hamdi access to a lawyer or to appear in person in court. Finally, the government provided to the court as evidence a declaration from a Defense Department official stating that Hamdi had traveled to Afghanistan in the summer of 2001, affiliated himself with a Taliban military unit, and surrendered while armed.

After proceedings in the district court and the Fourth Circuit, the case arrived before the Supreme Court on the question of whether the government could detain Hamdi as an enemy combatant. This raised the basic questions of whether the September 11 attacks constituted a war, which branch of the government had the authority to decide that question, and what powers were available to the president if, indeed, the United States were at war. If September 11, for example, merely constituted a criminal act rather than an act of war, then Hamdi's detention was illegal under the Fifth and Sixth Amendments, which require indictment or presentment, right to counsel, the right to remain silent, and the right to a speedy trial. Hamdi's detention also would have violated Section 4001(a), because no act of Congress has overridden the rights of criminal defendants to be free of detention without criminal charge.

A four-justice plurality opinion of the Court agreed with the government that the September 11 attacks had initiated a state of war, that the Afghanistan conflict was part of that war, and that enemy combatants could be detained without criminal charge as part of that war. As an initial matter, the Court avoided the Solicitor General's argument that the president could detain Hamdi pursuant solely to his authority, under Article II of the Constitution, to conduct war.[10]

10. *Id.* at 2639.

The Court could do so because Congress had enacted a statute on September 19, 2001, authorizing the president to use "all necessary and appropriate force" against "nations, organizations, or persons" he determines are responsible for the September 11 attacks. Agreement of the political branches that the September 11 attacks initiated a war and that the president could pursue that conflict in Afghanistan was enough to trigger deference on the part of the Court. "There can be no doubt that individuals who fought against the United States in Afghanistan as part of the Taliban, an organization known to have supported the al Qaeda terrorist network responsible for those attacks, are individuals Congress sought to target in passing" the authorization to use force.[11] The Court did not itself conduct any inquiry into whether the basic facts satisfied the statute or whether the statute satisfied the Constitution. It did not ask whether the September 11 attacks had indeed constituted an act of war for constitutional purposes; it did not ask whether sufficient evidence existed to show that al Qaeda was responsible for those attacks; nor did it examine whether the Taliban regime was sufficiently associated with al Qaeda to fall within the September 18 authorization.

Once the Court agreed that the September 11 attacks initiated a state of war with al Qaeda, it then accepted the next portion of the administration's legal framework for the war on terrorism. Ever since the earliest days of warfare, the lesser power to detain combatants has been understood to fall within the greater authority to use force against the enemy.[12] As the Court recognized, the purpose of detention in the military context is not to punish, but merely to prevent combatants from returning to the fight. In fact, such detention is the merciful, humanitarian alternative to a practice of granting no quarter to the enemy. That power extends even to U.S. citizens, as it did in the case of *Ex parte Quirin*, in which the Court upheld the World

11. *Id.* at 2640.
12. See, e.g., *Ex parte Quirin*, 317 U.S. 1, 28 (1942).

War II detention and trial by military commission of Nazi saboteurs, one of whom apparently was a U.S. citizen.[13] After noting that the laws of war permitted the detention without criminal charge of Confederate soldiers during the Civil War, the Court observed that "[a] citizen, no less than an alien, can be 'part of or supporting forces hostile to the United States or coalition partners' and 'engaged in an armed conflict against the United States.'"[14] No specific congressional authorization, the Court further concluded, was needed. "Because detention to prevent a combatant's return to the battlefield is a fundamental incident of waging war," the Court concluded, "in permitting the use of 'necessary and appropriate force'" Congress authorized wartime detention of enemy combatants.[15]

The Court finally upheld the third leg of the administration's justification for Hamdi's detention. Hamdi and his supporters argued that his detention was unconstitutional because it was indefinite—a return to the idea that terrorism constitutes a fundamentally criminal enterprise. Hamdi sought a return to September 10, 2001—when terrorists were arrested based on probable cause; were indicted by grand juries; received *Miranda* warnings, attorneys, a speedy trial, and the right to know all of the government's case, to depose and call any relevant witnesses, and to seek *Brady* evidence, among other things. The Court flatly rejected this argument. The justices recognized that the United States may use all of the tools of war to fight a new kind of enemy that has no territory, no population, and no desire to spare innocent civilian life. The days when terrorism was merely considered a law-enforcement problem and our only forces were limited to the FBI, federal prosecutors, and the criminal justice system will not be returning any time soon.

Instead, the Court drew upon the standard rule under the laws of war that prisoners can be detained until the end of a conflict. This

13. *Id.*
14. *Hamdi*, 124 S. Ct. at 2640–41.
15. *Id.* at 2641.

principle follows from the basic purposes of wartime detention of enemy combatants. As we have seen, to borrow the plurality's words, "the purpose of detention is to prevent captured individuals from returning to the field of battle and taking up arms once again."[16] The flip side of this purpose is that once a conflict is over, the relationship between the nations and populations returns to peace.[17] Once peace exists, no reason continues to exist for detaining captured combatants, and it becomes the obligation of each nation to prevent their citizens from restarting hostilities. "The United States may detain, for the duration of these hostilities, individuals legitimately determined to be Taliban combatants who 'engaged in an armed conflict against the United States.'"[18] So long as "the record establishes that United States troops are still involved in active combat in Afghanistan," detention may continue. The Court accepted the government's arguments that it was premature to identify when the conflict *might* end while combat operations in Afghanistan were still ongoing, as they are still ongoing today.

At the same time, the Court acknowledged the unconventional nature of the war on terrorism and suggested that if hostilities continued for "two generations," Hamdi's detention might indeed become indefinite and fall outside the government's war powers. Aside from recalling Justice O'Connor's fondness for measuring time by generations,[19] the Court did not provide any specific details about why thirty-six years ought to constitute any principled line. Suppose American troops remain engaged in combat in Afghanistan in 2040; nothing in the laws of war requires the United States to release Hamdi or other Taliban detainees. Even if Hamdi were no longer a threat

16. *Id.* at 2640.

17. Cf. Geneva Convention (III) Relative to the Treatment of Prisoners of War, art. 118, Aug. 12, 1949, 6 U.S.T. 3316, T.I.A.S. No. 3364; Hague Convention (II) on Laws and Customs of War on Land, art. 20, July 29, 1899, 32 Stat. 1817; Hague Convention (IV) of 1907, Oct. 18, 1907, 36 Stat. 2301.

18. *Hamdi*, 124 S. Ct. at 2642.

19. See *Grutter v. University of Michigan*, 539 U.S. 306, 343 (2003).

because of his age, harmlessness itself is not a grounds to seek release—nations at war, for example, are not required to release disabled prisoners of war. While the United States may decide to release older or less dangerous prisoners as a matter of policy, the Court identified no constitutional rule that required their release within a specific period of time not set by the end of hostilities.

Upholding detention as a central aspect of the war power is perhaps the most significant aspect of the Court's terrorism decisions. Afghanistan presents the easiest case: a traditional conflict between two nation-states that occurred primarily on the battlefield. It may be hard to believe, but the United States was lucky—al Qaeda and its Taliban allies chose to deploy fighters in a battlefield setting where superior American air and ground power gave the United States the advantage. Al Qaeda will not make that mistake twice. Rather, al Qaeda seeks to infiltrate operatives into our open society with the goal of launching surprise attacks designed to inflict massive civilian casualties. As the Jose Padilla example shows (whose case was dismissed by the Supreme Court because it was improperly brought in New York), al Qaeda has been recruiting American citizens who can better escape detection. Although fighting there continues, Afghanistan will not be the front line of the future; O'Hare airport, New York harbor, and the Mexican and Canadian borders will be. Preventing the government from detaining citizens who have decided to become terrorists would have seriously handicapped the nation's ability to stop attacks and to gain better intelligence on our enemy's plans.

III.

Up to this point, the Court remained well within the bounds set by previous Courts in reviewing government war powers to detain enemy combatants. At the outset of the Civil War, for example, the Court had deferred to the president's determination of whether a war had broken out with the Confederacy. In *The Prize Cases*, the Court explained that "[w]hether the President in fulfilling his duties as Commander in Chief" was justified in treating the southern States as belligerents and instituting a blockade, was a question "to be *decided by him*."[20] The Court could not question the merits of his decision, but must leave evaluation to "the political department of the Government to which this power was entrusted."[21] As the Court observed, the president enjoys full discretion in determining what level of force to use.[22] At the end of World War II, the Court had found that the question of whether a state of war continued in existence despite the apparent cessation of active military operations was a political question.[23] In the first years of World War II, the Court upheld the government's authority to detain enemy combatants, even citizens, during war. Despite the arguments of a coalition of law professors, members of the bar, and commentators, in *Hamdi*, it would have been remarkable for the Court to have disregarded this framework developed over the nation's long history and to have challenged the political branches in perhaps their area of greatest competence.[24]

It was at this point, however, that the Court then took a wrong turn and overstepped the traditional boundaries of judicial review. All

20. *The Prize Cases*, 67 U.S. (2 Black) 635, 670 (1862).

21. *Id.*

22. *Id.* ("He must determine what degree of force the crisis demands.") (internal quotations omitted); see *Eisentrager*, 339 U.S. 763, 789 (1950) ("Certainly it is not the function of the Judiciary to entertain private litigation—even by a citizen—which challenges the legality, the wisdom, or the propriety of the Commander-in-Chief in sending our armed forces abroad or to any particular region."); *Chicago & S. Air Lines v. Waterman Steamship Corp.*, 333 U.S. 103, 111 (1948) ("The President, both as Commander-in-Chief and as the Nation's organ for foreign affairs, has available intelligence services whose reports are not and ought not to be published to the world. It would be intolerable that courts, without the relevant information, should review and perhaps nullify actions of the Executive taken on information properly held secret.").

23. *Ludecke v. Watkins*, 335 U.S. 160, 167–70 (1948).

24. It is important to note that although Justice O'Connor's opinion drew only a plurality of the Court—Chief Justice Rehnquist and Justices Kennedy and Breyer— Justice Thomas's dissent agreed with the plurality on these essential points.

parties agreed that an American citizen held as an enemy combatant could challenge his detention through a petition for a writ of habeas corpus. This had been the rule since at least *Ex parte Milligan* (1866), in which the Court ordered the release of an American citizen who had plotted to attack military installations and was detained by Union military authorities while "the courts are open and their process unobstructed."[25] Milligan had been captured well away from the front, had never associated with the enemy, and at best was merely a sympathizer with the Confederate cause.[26] The crucial question, then, was not whether habeas corpus would remain available but how the process ought to be structured to take into account the government's interests in protecting the national security and the noncriminal nature of the detention, while at the same time providing a sufficient test of the government's evidence to guard against pretextual detentions.

Viewed at a somewhat higher level of generality, *Hamdi* really called upon the Court to determine how much information judges need to perform the habeas function in a wartime detention context. In a regular habeas case, for example, a federal court reviewing a purely executive detention (rather than, as is usually the case, detention and conviction of a criminal defendant by the state courts) might exercise de novo review of the facts. If the executive claimed, for example, that an individual had to be detained because he posed an imminent threat to public safety, a judge might feel it necessary to examine witnesses in court and to directly review the records of the detention.[27] Or, following Judge Wilkinson's approach in the Fourth Circuit, the Court could have accepted the "some evidence" standard

25. *Ex parte Milligan*, 71 U.S. (4 Wall.) 2, 121 (1866).
26. *Id.* at 131.
27. See, e.g., *United States v. Salerno*, 481 U.S. 739, 748 (1987) ("in times of war or insurrection, when society's interest is at its peak, the Government may detain individuals whom the government believes to be dangerous."); *Moyer v. Peabody*, 212 U.S. 78, 82–83 (1909) (governor's detention of individual because of insurrection).

that required the government to provide the facts that led the military to believe that a detainee satisfies the legal standard for status as an enemy combatant. That standard seeks to provide the government the maximum flexibility to preserve its intelligence sources and methods and to minimize interference with ongoing military operations. Such considerations had led the Court in 1950 to refuse to allow alien enemy combatants resort to habeas at all. In *Eisentrager*, the Court had held that German POWs convicted by military commission for war crimes could not seek review of their sentences in a federal court through a writ of habeas corpus. According to the *Eisentrager* Court:

> The writ, since it is held to be a matter of right, would be equally available to enemies during active hostilities as in the present twilight between war and peace. Such trials would hamper the war effort and bring aid and comfort to the enemy. They would diminish the prestige of our commanders, not only with enemies but with wavering neutrals. It would be difficult to devise a more effective fettering of a field commander than to allow the very enemies he is ordered to reduce to submission to call him to account in his own civil courts and divert his efforts and attention from the military offensive abroad to the legal defensive at home. Nor is it unlikely that the result of such enemy litigiousness would be a conflict between judicial and military opinion highly comforting to enemies of the United States.[28]

Add to these concerns the important military interest, only made more acute by the unconventional nature of the war with al Qaeda, of interrogating enemy combatants for information about coming attacks. Unlike previous wars, the current enemy is a stateless network of religious extremists who do not obey the laws of war, who hide among peaceful populations, and who seek to launch surprise attacks on civilian targets with the aim of causing massive casualties. They have no armed forces to target, no territory to defend, no people to protect, and no fear of killing themselves in their attacks. The front

28. *Eisentrager*, 339 U.S. at 779.

line is not solely a traditional battlefield, and the primary means of conducting the war includes the efforts of military, law enforcement, and intelligence officers to stop attacks *before* they occur. Information is the primary weapon in the conflict against this new kind of enemy, and intelligence gathered from captured operatives is perhaps the most effective means of preventing future terrorist attacks upon U.S. territory.

According to this understanding of war, de novo judicial review threatened to undermine the very effectiveness of the military effort against al Qaeda. A habeas proceeding could become the forum for recalling commanders and intelligence operatives from the field into open court; disrupting overt and covert operations; revealing successful military tactics and methods; and forcing the military to shape its activities to the demands of the judicial process. Indeed, the discovery orders of the trial judge in *Hamdi* threatened to achieve exactly these results. Appropriate concern over these considerations should have led the Court to adopt the "some evidence" standard, which promised to narrow judicial inquiry to the facts known to the government and subject to production in court. Justice Thomas, who observed that courts "lack the expertise and capacity to second-guess" the battlefield decisions made by the military and ultimately the president, agreed with this approach.

Joined by Justices Souter and Ginsburg, however, the plurality imposed vague guidelines for reviewing detentions. Rejecting the positions of both Hamdi and the government, it struck the compromise that an enemy combatant must receive a lawyer and "a fair opportunity to rebut the Government's factual assertions before a neutral decisionmaker." It transplanted that most amorphous of standards—the *Mathews v. Eldridge's* test—to determine whether a process meets the requirement of the due process clause: a balancing of the private interest affected by government action, the government's interests, and the costs of providing greater process, all measured in the context of deciding whether more process would reduce government error.[29] That the Court had to resort to a case about the procedural due process rights that attend the termination of welfare benefits suggests the extent to which the Court was improvising.

It is difficult to understand how the *Eldridge* test can be applied with any serious coherence. The values that *Eldridge* calls on the courts to balance seem obviously difficult, if not impossible, to measure against any common metric. The Court's own discussion in *Hamdi* bears this out. On the one hand, Justice O'Connor wrote that an individual citizen's interest "to be free from involuntary confinement by his own government" is fundamental.[30] On the other hand, the government has a "weighty and sensitive" interest in preventing enemy combatants from returning to fight against the United States.[31] The Court could have defined the government's interest at an even higher level of importance, because requiring the government to reveal intelligence information, such as the surveillance of al Qaeda leaders, during habeas proceedings could prevent the government from carrying out the shadowy war against al Qaeda with its most effective sources and methods. Once defined as prevailing in the conflict, rather than simply detaining enemy combatants, the government's interest would have reached the most compelling level known to American constitutional law. As the Court has said before, "It is 'obvious and unarguable' that no governmental interest is more compelling than the security of the Nation."[32]

Nevertheless, how the Court actually measures these factors is unclear, especially so in the Court's opinion. Do we gauge the government's interest in protecting the national security in lives potentially saved times the reduction in the probability of an attack— factoring in the average value of a life as measured by the Department of Health and Human Services or the Environmental Protection

29. *Mathews v. Eldridge*, 424 U.S. 319, 335 (1976).
30. *Hamdi*, 124 S. Ct. at 2647.
31. *Id.*
32. *Haig v. Agee*, 453 U.S. 280, 307 (1981) (citation omitted).

Agency? And how does the government measure the individual liberty interest against unwilling detention—in the average amount of dollars that an average citizen would pay to avoid detention per hour? If these efforts to monetarize the values seem silly, then perhaps we can admit there is no systematic, rational way to balance these competing values. Then, to make matters even more difficult, the Court requires that judges use these values as guideposts with which to determine which procedural features should attend habeas corpus proceedings for enemy combatants. Even though it made various observations about possible procedures—such as suggesting that the government should receive a presumption in favor of its evidence, one that put the burden of proof on the detainee to disprove—the Court really just punted on the procedures to the lower courts and the executive branch.

One might think of *Hamdi* as a case in which its practical importance outstrips its significance as a matter of theory or policy. After all, the government had detained only three American citizens as enemy combatants, Yaser Hamdi, John Walker Lindh, and Jose Padilla. As of this writing, Lindh was transferred to the criminal justice system and reached a plea bargain with prosecutors, while Hamdi has renounced his citizenship and been released to the custody of Saudi Arabia. *Hamdi*, however, has application far beyond the remaining case of Padilla because of the Court's decision in *Rasul v. Bush*, in which the Court found that Guantanamo Bay (and perhaps military operations worldwide) lay within the jurisdiction of the federal courts. *Rasul* essentially overruled *Eisentrager*, and it unwisely threatens to inject the federal courts into the micromanagement of the military. *Rasul* provided no guidance on how soon those hearings must be held, where they will be held, who can participate, and how classified intelligence will remain protected. Despite an extended discussion of the peculiarities of the Guantanamo lease, *Rasul* even leaves unclear whether judicial review would apply beyond the Guantanamo base to Iraq (and Saddam Hussein) or Afghanistan (and Osama bin Laden, should he be captured).

Without any discussion of these issues in *Rasul*, we can only assume that the approach outlined in *Hamdi* will prove sufficient to meet habeas corpus standards. If the process is sufficient to meet the due process standards for American citizens detained within the United States, it seems safe to conclude that they will satisfy the requirements for alien enemy combatants detained outside the United States. Although it unwisely extended its reach to wartime detentions outside the United States, the Court left the executive branch with substantial room to maneuver on the nature and scope of review. *Hamdi*, for example, approves of a detainee's access to counsel, but it does not explain when they can meet, whether their communications can be monitored for clandestine messages, or whether the lawyers can be military officers. *Rasul* studiously avoided any discussion of the substantive rights, if any, that al Qaeda and Taliban detainees have, and neither decision overturned the administration's policy that the Geneva Conventions do not apply. The Pentagon could easily adapt its existing review process for Guantanamo prisoners to meet the standards of *Hamdi* (as Justice O'Connor seemed to invite). Military commissions already established by President Bush to try alien terrorists would almost certainly meet the procedural requirements set out by the Court. Thus, the Court's intervention into detainee policy, and its imposition of ambiguous standards for review, threaten to extend not just to the navy brig in Charleston, South Carolina, but also to Guantanamo Bay, Afghanistan, and even Iraq.

IV.

Despite protests to the contrary, *Hamdi* and *Rasul* will thrust the federal courts into the center of policy making in the war on terrorism. The courts will face decisions about whether the government must produce certain kinds of evidence or witnesses, particularly those involving intelligence information and assets; how long the government can question detained enemy combatants before they have access to a lawyer; and how much the government must disclose in open court about its operations. These decisions will have an effect on the tactics and operations that the government will be able to use to combat terrorism in the future. Because the Court did not set any clear lines, but instead called on lower courts to balance multiple factors, it is hard to escape the conclusion that the federal judiciary will have a significant policy-making role on terrorism issues. This part of the chapter questions whether the courts have a comparative advantage in the area of foreign policy and national security, or whether such decisions should be left to the political branches. Do the federal courts, now charged with interpreting and applying *Hamdi* and *Rasul*, have a superior ability to gather information to make national security decisions or even to conduct the balancing called for by the Supreme Court?

The design and operation of the judiciary give it a comparatively weak institutional vantage point from which to achieve foreign affairs and national security goals. This is not to say that federal courts are institutionally unable to play a role. Rather, the important question for ensuring the most effective pursuit of national policy is, Which institutions within the federal government have a comparative advantage as a matter of their structure? As to this second-order question, I argue that the federal judiciary, in such a role, suffers significant institutional disadvantages that make it a poor choice for carrying out national security policy. It is important to distinguish between both micro and macro level characteristics of the judiciary. Several characteristics of federal courts at the micro level—the operation of individual judges in individual lawsuits—limit the information that flows to courts and the options available to them. At a macro level, certain systemwide features of the Article III judiciary may poorly equip it to carry out national policy on a global scale.

1. Micro factors

The defining function and features of the Article III courts, which may make them superior to other branches in performing certain functions, also may make them comparatively less well suited to playing a leading national security role. Federal courts are designed to be independent from politics, to passively allow parties to drive the litigation, and to receive information in highly formal ways through litigation. These characteristics may make courts more neutral in their decision making and fairer in their attitude toward defendants or detainees. But they also may render the courts less effective tools for achieving national security goals. Comparison of courts with other institutions may make these points more salient.

An initial difference between courts and other institutions is access. Compared with other institutions, courts have high barriers to access from parties.[33] Markets, to take one example, have virtually no barriers—all one need do is purchase a product. Congress has somewhat higher barriers than markets. It is generally thought that interest groups must provide campaign contributions or political support in order to attain access to political leaders, although studies also show that members of Congress are responsive to public pressure as reflected through the media and constituents.[34] The executive branch has lower levels of access than Congress; it is probably easier for individuals and groups to provide information to, and make requests of, agencies, although perhaps with no greater chances of success than with Congress. Certainly, for members of Congress, access to the executive branch is extremely low. In addition to formal hearings and information transmitted to Congress by the executive branch, agency officials and congressional staff conduct numerous discussions

33. NEIL KOMESAR, IMPERFECT ALTERNATIVES: CHOOSING INSTITUTIONS IN LAW, ECONOMICS, AND PUBLIC POLICY 125 (1994).
34. See ROBERT COOTER, THE STRATEGIC CONSTITUTION 51–74 (1999) (discussing interest group theory of politics).

and meetings in a never-ending dialogue of questions and requests for information and responses.[35]

By contrast, courts have numerous doctrines that limit access to the courtroom. Under standing doctrine, for example, plaintiffs must have suffered an actual injury in fact, which is traceable to conduct on the part of a defendant who can remedy the harm.[36] The timing of the case must be just right, neither too early to be unripe nor too late to be moot.[37] Of particular importance to the subject matter at hand, the case cannot raise political questions whose determination is constitutionally vested in another branch.[38] The plaintiff must actually be able to claim to benefit from a cause of action created under federal law. Litigation itself demands significant resources, at least in comparison with means of accessing the executive or legislative branches. Taking advantage of a judicial forum not only requires time and money to make substantive legal arguments in court and to pursue discovery, but also demands resources for navigating the complexity of litigation rules—hence, the need to hire teams of lawyers to represent parties in interest.

There are also significant differences in the manner by which courts acquire and process information. Information is gathered through a painstaking process of discovery, conducted between the contending parties, which can take a long time and incur great expense. That information must satisfy the federal rules of evidence—it must survive tests for relevance, credibility, and reliability—and it must be presented to the court in accordance with specific, fairly painstaking courtroom procedures. The executive branch, by contrast, can collect information through agency experts, a national and global

---

35. See, e.g., Peter Strauss, *The Place of Agencies in the Government: Separation of Powers and the Fourth Branch*, 84 COLUM. L. REV. 573 (1984).

36. See, e.g., *Lujan v. Defenders of Wildlife*, 504 U.S. 555 (1992).

37. See, e.g., *DeFunis v. Odegaard*, 416 U.S. 312 (1974) (mootness); *United Public Workers v. Mitchell*, 330 U.S. 75 (1947) (ripeness).

38. *Nixon v. United States*, 506 U.S. 224 (1993).

network of officials and agents, and links with outside groups and foreign governments. Congress can collect information itself or acquire it from the executive branch or outside groups via relatively inexpensive hearings. Courts, however, cannot proactively collect information on a question before them. Aside from public record information, such as that contained in open media sources or scholarly journals, courts must rely on the parties to bring information to them. Courts do not operate the broad network of information sources available to the executive branch, nor can they benefit from the informal methods of information collection at the disposal of the legislature. Indeed, courts usually cannot update the information available on a question except through the context of a case. Thus, if a court has made a decision based on information available to it at time 1, it usually will not continue to gather information thereafter—even if that information gathering would lead it to change its decision—until another case raising the same issue is brought. And even then, a court usually will not reexamine its earlier decision unless the information provided by the parties showed that the factual context has changed so dramatically as to dictate a departure from stare decisis.[39]

Article III itself also imposes significant restrictions on the role of courts in performing certain functions. Once the president and Congress have enacted a statute, the judiciary's constitutional responsibility is to execute those goals in the context of Article III cases or controversies, subject to any policy-making discretion that the courts are implicitly given by Congress in areas of statutory ambiguity or of federal common law. Federal judges cannot alter or refuse to execute those policies, even if the original circumstances that gave rise to the statute have changed.[40] If a federal court, for example, finds that a

39. See, e.g., Thomas R. Lee, *Stare Decisis in Economic Perspective: An Economic Analysis of the Supreme Court's Doctrine of Precedent*, 78 N.C. L. Rev. 643 (2000).

40. For a contrary view, see GUIDO CALABRESI, A COMMON LAW FOR THE AGE OF STATUTES (1985).

92 JOHN YOO

defendant has violated the Helms-Burton Act by "trafficking" in property confiscated by the Cuban government, it must render judgment for an American plaintiff who once owned that property.[41] Article III requires a federal court to reach that decision, even if the effects of the judgment in that particular case would actually harm the national interest. This is because courts cannot control the timing of their proceedings or coordinate their judgments with the actions of the other branches of government. One might easily see how this might be the case: The president, for example, might be engaged in a diplomatic campaign to pressure a Middle Eastern country into terminating its support for terrorism at the time that a judicial decision frees a suspected al Qaeda operative. A judicial decision along these lines could undermine the appearance of unified resolve on the part of the United States, or it might suggest to the Middle Eastern country that the executive branch could not guarantee that it could follow through on its own counterterrorism policies. A court cannot take account of such naked policy considerations in deciding whether a federal statute has been violated or whether to grant relief, whereas the political branches, of course, can make constant policy modifications in reaction to ongoing events.

A last micro difficulty arises from the substantive challenge presented by international law. Detention decisions will call on the federal courts not only to find facts in applying the enemy combatant standard; they may also have to hear claims brought by detainees that their treatment or conditions of confinement violate international treaties or customary international law or that the manner of their capture violated international law. International law is a very different subject from that usually encountered by federal courts. Many observers admit that the very concept of customary international law—law that "results from a general and consistent practice of states followed

41. John Yoo, *Federal Courts as Weapons of Foreign Policy: The Case of the Helms-Burton Act*, 20 HASTINGS INT'L & COMP. L. REV. 747 (1997).

by them from a sense of legal obligation" rather than through positive enactment[42]—is fraught with difficulty.[43]

Even if the very nature of international law were not so uncertain and ambiguous, it is likely that the federal courts would either experience a high error rate in determining its content or expend high decision costs to attempt to reach the right answer. International law involves sources that are not often encountered by federal judges or American lawyers. The very source of customary international law—state practice—is not as readily available to courts as are reported decisions. State practice may not even be reflected in publicly available documents, but may more often lie in the archives of the State Department and foreign ministries, or they may not even be recorded in documents at all, but rest in the preserve of unwritten custom. American-trained judges—almost all of them generalists—would have to survey the actions of governments over the course of dozens, if not hundreds, of years and make fine-grained judgments not just about what states have done but also why they did it.

An analogy here can be made to the disputes over the use of legislative history in statutory interpretation. Whether courts should consult legislative history has proven to be one of the focal points for broader debates about the nature of the legislation, the process of judicial reasoning, and the purpose of interpretation. To summarize all too briefly, many who believe that courts should seek out Congress's "intent" or broader "purpose" find reliance on legislative history, along with other policy considerations, generally acceptable.[44]

---

42. Restatement (Third) of the Foreign Relations Law of the United States § 102(2) (1987).

43. Compare ANTHONY A. D'AMATO, THE CONCEPT OF CUSTOM IN INTERNATIONAL LAW 4 (1971) with IAN BROWNLIE, PRINCIPLES OF PUBLIC INTERNATIONAL LAW 5–6 (4th ed., 1990).

44. See, e.g., William N. Eskridge Jr., *Textualism, the Unknown Ideal?* 96 MICH. L. REV. 1509 (1998) (reviewing ANTONIN SCALIA, A MATTER OF INTERPRETATION: FEDERAL COURTS AND THE LAW (1997)); Daniel A. Farber and Philip P. Frickey, *Legislative Intent and Public Choice*, 74 VA. L. REV. 423 (1988); William N. Eskridge

A minority argue that legislative history ought not to be used, either because there is no such thing as a collective intent or because consulting legislative history evades the formal separation of powers.[45] Adrian Vermeule made a similar argument in this debate: Even if courts should seek legislative intent, their "limited interpretive competence" suggests that they "might do better, even on intentionalist grounds, by eschewing legislative history than by consulting it."[46] Judges simply may have limited competence in understanding and properly using legislative history, leading both to high decision costs in conducting extensive reviews of legislative history without any corresponding reduction (and perhaps even an increase) in error costs.

If this is true with regard to legislative history, these costs will only be compounded in the context of international law. The sources of legislative history at least rest within the general bounds of American public law, and so will be familiar to most judges. Although expensive to gather and analyze in relation to other forms of American legal research,[47] legislative history may well be cheap to use in comparison with sources of international law, which comes in different languages, involves not just texts but also practices, and is recorded in sources that are often not publicly available. Even the use of more conventional public sources, such as multilateral treaties and the resolutions of the UN General Assembly, have serious interpretive problems. It is highly questionable, for example, that nations that refuse to sign treaties should be held to the same norms because

---

Jr. and Philip P. Frickey, *Statutory Interpretation as Practical Reasoning*, 42 STAN. L. REV. 321 (1990).

45. See, e.g., John F. Manning, *Textualism as a Nondelegation Doctrine*, 97 COLUM. L. REV. 673 (1997); Frank H. Easterbrook, *Text, History, and Structure in Statutory Interpretation*, 17 HARV. J. L. & PUB. POL'Y, 61, 68 (1994).

46. See Adrian Vermeule, *Legislative History and the Limits of Judicial Competence: The Untold Story of* Holy Trinity Church, 50 STAN. L. REV. 1833 (1998).

47. See, e.g., Kenneth W. Starr, *Observations About the Use of Legislative History*, DUKE L. J. 371, 377 (1987); Eskridge, supra note 44, at 1541; Vermeule, supra note 46, at 1868–69.

they have "ripened" into custom or that customary international law should be read to go beyond the standards set by a widely joined treaty. Decisions by organs of the United Nations, particularly of the General Assembly, have no formal authority in declaring customary international law if, by definition, that law represents the practice of *states*, not the opinions of international organizations.[48] The most pertinent evidence of state practice will be the most expensive to come by, and there is no empirical showing yet that federal courts will perform better in their use than any other institution.

2. Macro institutional factors

The organization of the federal judiciary as an institution perhaps has even more significant effects on the comparative ability of the courts to achieve national security goals. First, the federal judiciary is a generalist institution composed of generalist judges. Members of the judiciary are not often chosen because of expertise in any particular subject—unlike, say, the way in which scientists may be hired for work at the Department of Energy, the Environmental Protection Agency, or the Food and Drug Administration. This is even more so the case in foreign affairs; judges are usually not chosen because of any background in specific regions or areas, nor are they selected because they have experience in national security issues. As an institution, the judiciary is unlikely to have great facility with international legal, political, or economic theories or materials, and its members are more likely to be chosen because of their prominence as litigators or as public officials. It is difficult to remember more than a handful

---

48. The legitimacy of this "new" customary international law is debated in Prosper Weil, *Toward Relative Normativity in International Law?* 77 AM. J. INT'L L. 413, 433 (1983); Alain Pellet, *The Normative Dilemma: Will and Consent in International Lawmaking*, 12 AUSTRALIAN Y.B. INT'L L. 22 (1992), and is summarized in ANTONIO CASSESE AND JOSEPH H. H. WEILER (eds.), CHANGE AND STABILITY IN INTERNATIONAL LAWMAKING (1988). For discussions of the problems with international law raised here, see generally Patrick Kelly, *The Twilight of Customary International Law*, 40 VA. J. INT'L L. 449 (2000).

of judges who had significant foreign affairs experience before their appointment to the federal bench, and certainly a candidate's prominence in the field of public international law or international relations theory would not be a strong selling point for a nominee.

Similarly, the federal judiciary itself is organized along generalist lines. Aside from the Court of Appeals for the Federal Circuit, the federal courts are organized by geographic region, not by subject matter in the way that some European judicial systems are. This not only prevents specialization, but it also retards the accumulation of experience and the easy internal transmission of information between judges handling common issues. Few judges will have any special background, for example, in arms control issues, and even if some gain significant knowledge about it through a particular case, the generalist organization of the judiciary means that this experience will not be retained and put to use in all future cases on the same subjects. In fact, it is highly unlikely those judges will hear cases on the same subject again.

Second, of the three branches of government, the judiciary is the most decentralized. It can lay claim to being the most balkanized, if also the most deliberate. The front line of the judiciary is composed of ninety-four district courts, which are staffed by more than 667 judges.[49] Until appellate courts have ruled on a legal issue, the judges in these district courts can hold ninety-four different interpretations of the law. There are thirteen federal courts of appeals, with 179 judges.[50] The Supreme Court currently hears between seventy and eighty-five cases per year, while about 60,000 cases a year are filed in the Courts of Appeal and about 325,000 cases are filed each year in the district courts.[51] Given the other demands on the Supreme

49. History of Federal Judgeships, U.S. District Courts, http://www.uscourts.gov/history/tableh.pdf.

50. History of Federal Judgeships, U.S. Courts of Appeals, http://www.uscourts.gov/history/tablec.pdf.

51. Judicial Caseload Indicators 2003, http://www.uscourts.gov/caseload2003/front/Mar03Txt.pdf.

Court's caseload, it is doubtful that the Court could devote a significant portion of its docket to correcting erroneous interpretation of international law or mistaken interference with foreign and national security policy set by the political branches. Unless this happens, the geographic organization of the federal courts may well produce disharmony or at least an undesirable diversity of possible interpretations and applications of international law and foreign policy.

In some areas, this level of decentralization might not pose such a problem. Geographically organized courts may better tailor national policies to local conditions, allow for diversity and even experimentation in federal policies, and provide a more effective voice for local communities in federal judicial decision making. These are not positive values, however, in foreign affairs and national security. The Constitution specifically sought to centralize authority over these subjects to provide the nation with a single voice in its international relations, so as to prevent other nations from taking advantage of the disarray that had characterized the Articles of Confederation.[52] Indeed, in cases such as *Crosby* and *Garamendi*, the Court recently has preempted state efforts to influence the conduct of foreign nations precisely because of the need for a uniform foreign policy set by the Congress or the president.[53] This rationale, however, which was offered to justify national preeminence over the fifty states, applies with equal force to a federal judiciary of ninety-four district courts and thirteen appellate courts. The usual factors that have led to judicial specialization do not seem to be present here. Unlike the Second Circuit and securities law, there is no natural geographic center for matters that affect international relations, and unlike the D.C. Circuit and administrative law, the habeas corpus statute does not require that detainee suits be brought in a specific court of appeals. In fact,

---

52. See generally FREDERICK MARKS, INDEPENDENCE ON TRIAL: FOREIGN AFFAIRS AND THE MAKING OF THE CONSTITUTION (1973).

53. *American Insurance Association v. Garamendi*, 539 U.S. 396 (2003); *Crosby v. National Foreign Trade Council*, 530 U.S. 363 (2000).

Rasul seems to suggest that enemy combatants held outside the United States could bring suits in any of the federal district courts. Judicial implementation of foreign and national security policy seems to bring a promise of disharmony where uniformity is perhaps supremely important.

Third, institutional structure also suggests that judicial activity in national security may be slow, in terms of both implementation and self-correction. Lawsuits can often take years to complete. Even when cases are expedited, they will certainly require several months to complete from time of filing to final judgment and appeal. Even though they did not reach extensive discovery or trial proceedings, recent Supreme Court cases on Massachusetts' efforts to sanction Burma and on California's efforts to provide remedies for Holocaust victims still took several years to adjudicate.[54] Last term's enemy combatant cases—in which the legal issues were clear, no discovery was needed, and detainees had significant liberty interests in a swift resolution—still required roughly two to three years for decision on the threshold substantive questions.[55] These cases may even have proceeded quickly by judicial standards, but the important question is whether, as a matter of comparative institutional competence, the executive or other branches can implement foreign policy goals even faster.

Delay also may be the story of the day with regard to monitoring and feedback. Judicial errors or deviations from policy may take years to reverse or may even go entirely uncorrected. Stories about the delay between the filing of a suit in federal court and the eventual judgment are well known. Slowness obviously impedes the swift and effective execution of foreign policy. Delay also infects the judiciary's institu-

54. The lawsuit in *Garamendi* began in 1999 and was not finally decided by the Supreme Court until 2003 (124 S. Ct. at 2385). *Crosby* began in 1998 and was not decided by the Supreme Court until 2000 (530 U.S. at 371).

55. See, e.g., *Hamdi*, 124 S.Ct. at 2636 (Hamdi captured in 2001; habeas filed in 2002); *Rasul*, 124 S.Ct. at 2691 (detainees captured in 2001; habeas filed in 2002).

tional systems for communicating between its different units and for correcting errors. Even though the federal courts have an appeals court system for detecting and correcting errors, it can take months, if not years, to run its course. Even if a district or circuit judge acts in defiance of established circuit court or Supreme Court precedent, litigation is needed to correct the error. Standards of review concerning fact finding may even render some decisions immune from appellate review, despite contrary or conflicting results reached by different trial courts in similar cases. Transmission of information identifying and correcting errors may become garbled within the system, which helps explain the repeated cycles of repeal and remand that can occur in the context of a single case.[56]

The judiciary's characteristics as an institution render it superior to other institutions for certain kinds of decisions. It can address issues more fairly and with less interference from the political branches, and it can implement federal policy over a wide number of cases throughout the country. Its high level of insulation from outside control allows it to help solve political commitment problems between interest groups or between branches of government. Its virtues, however, also create its problems as an institutional actor in foreign affairs and national security. Its evenhandedness and passivity create problems in gathering and processing information effectively and in coordinating its policies with other national actors. Its procedural fairness and geographic decentralization prevent it from acting swiftly in a unified fashion, and it lacks effective tools for the rapid assimilation of feedback and the correction of errors.

All of this is not to say that the federal courts should be utterly removed from the review of the detention of American citizens as enemy combatants. *Hamdi* is on the books, and the Supreme Court has decided *Rasul* and essentially overruled *Eisentrager*, which I think

---

56. Martin Shapiro, *Toward a Theory of Stare Decisis*, 1 J. LEG. STUD. 125, 125–34 (1972).

will prove to be mistaken. The federal courts *will* play a role in making terrorism policy, unless Congress and the president cooperate and enact a new habeas statute to govern enemy combatant cases (which appears unlikely so far). Nevertheless, these decisions provide to the lower courts fairly broad discretion in shaping procedures. Choices still must be made about the timing of detainees' access to lawyers, whether *Miranda* rights will be invoked, what evidence must be produced, whether witnesses must appear, and what standard of review should be applied to the military's decisions. Decisions still must be made about the deference, if any, that courts will provide to the executive's interpretation and application of international law, such as the Geneva Conventions. Even if the Court has rejected the "some evidence" test, it still might adopt the deference afforded to agency decision making under the arbitrary and capricious standard and *Chevron*.[57]

These decisions to come will fall on a spectrum between outright de novo review according to standards similar to those of the criminal justice system and a standard that would be deferential to the political branches. The analysis here seeks to point out the institutional difficulties that the courts will encounter in attempting to play a de novo role in reviewing national security decisions during the war on terrorism. All too often these decisions are characterized in terms of the policy goal sought, without regard to the second-order question of relative institutional capabilities. Rather than ask itself whether it can balance security against liberty interests—obviously it can choose some point on the policy spectrum—the judiciary ought to ask itself whether the other branches could strike a better balance based on more informed judgment. Given the micro and macro institutional problems with courts, the judiciary may undermine, rather than promote, national policy in the war on terrorism by overestimating its abilities and refusing to provide deference to the political branches.

57. *Chevron U.S.A., Inc. v. Natural Resources Defense Council, Inc.*, 467 U.S. 837 (1984) (judicial deference to agency interpretation of ambiguous law).

4. Judicial Baby-Splitting and the Failure of the Political Branches

Benjamin Wittes

The day the Supreme Court handed down what have collectively become known as the enemy combatant cases—June 28, 2004—was both widely anticipated and widely received as a legal moment of truth for the Bush administration's war on terrorism. The stakes could not have been higher. The three cases came down in the midst of election-year politics. They each involved challenges by detainees being held by the military without charge or trial or access to counsel. They each divided the Court. And they appeared to validate or reject core arguments that the administration had advanced—and had been slammed for advancing—since the fight against al Qaeda began in earnest after September 11, 2001.

The dominant view saw the cases as a major defeat for President George W. Bush—and with good reason. After all, his administration had urged the Court to refrain from asserting jurisdiction over the Guantanamo Bay naval base in Cuba, and it did just that in unambiguous terms: "Aliens held at the base, no less than American citizens, are entitled to invoke the federal courts' authority."[1] The administration fought tooth and nail for the proposition that an American citizen held domestically as an enemy combatant has no right to counsel and no right to respond to the factual assertions that justify his detention. The Court, however, held squarely that "a citizen-detainee seeking to challenge his classification as an enemy combatant must receive notice of the factual basis for his classification, and a fair opportunity to rebut the Government's factual assertions before a neutral decisionmaker."[2] It held as well that "[h]e unquestionably has the right to access to counsel" in doing so.[3] These holdings led the *New York Times* to call the cases "a stinging rebuke" to the administration's policies, one that "made it clear that even during the war on terror, the government must adhere to the rule of law."[4]

A dissident analysis of the cases, however, quickly emerged as well and saw them as a kind of victory for the administration dressed up in defeat's borrowed robes. As David B. Rivkin Jr. and Lee A. Casey put it: In the context of these cases, the court accepted the following critical propositions: that the United States is engaged in a legally cognizable armed conflict with al Qaeda and the Taliban, to which the laws of war apply; that "enemy combatants" captured in the context of that conflict can be held "indefinitely" without criminal trial while that conflict continues; that American citizens (at least those captured overseas) can be classified and detained as enemy combatants, confirming the authority of the court's 1942 decision in *Ex Parte Quirin* (the "Nazi saboteur" case); and that the role of the courts in reviewing such designations is limited. All these points had been disputed by one or more of the detainees' lawyers, and all are now settled in the government's favor.[5]

1. *Rasul v. Bush*, 124 S. Ct. 2686, 2696 (2004).
2. *Hamdi v. Rumsfeld*, 124 S. Ct. 2633, 2648 (2004).
3. *Id.* at 2652.
4. Editorial, "Reaffirming the Rule of Law," *New York Times*, June 29, 2003, A26.
5. David B. Rivkin Jr. and Lee A. Casey, "Bush's Good Day in Court," *Wash-*

Even among those who celebrated the administration's defeat, this analysis had some resonance. Ronald Dworkin, for example, began his essay on the cases by triumphantly declaring, "The Supreme Court has finally and decisively rejected the Bush administration's outrageous claim that the President has the power to jail people he accuses of terrorist connections without access to lawyers or the outside world and without any possibility of significant review by courts or other judicial bodies." But he then went on to acknowledge that the Court had "suggested rules of procedure for any such review that omit important traditional protections for people accused of crimes" and that the government "may well be able to satisfy the Court's lenient procedural standards without actually altering its morally dubious detention policies."[6] How big a rebuke could the cases really represent if they collectively entitle the president to stay the course he has chosen?

In my view, both strains of initial thought have considerable merit. The administration clearly suffered a "stinging rebuke" in rhetorical terms. But Dworkin, Rivkin, and Casey (an unlikely meeting of the minds if ever there were one) were quite correct that, in the long run, the president's actual power to detain enemy combatants may not have been materially damaged either with respect to citizens domestically or with respect to enemy fighters captured and held abroad. In a profound sense, the Supreme Court, despite delivering itself of 178 pages of text on the subject of enemy combatant detentions, managed to leave all of the central questions unanswered. In fact, if a new front in the war on terrorism opened tomorrow and the military captured a new crop of captives, under the Court's rulings, the administration would face very nearly the same questions as it did in 2002. Can the military warehouse foreign citizens captured

<hr>

ington Post, August 4, 2004, A19. The quotation refers to *Ex parte Quirin*, 317 U.S. 1 (1942).

6. Ronald Dworkin, "What the Court Really Said," *The New York Review of Books*, August 12, 2004.

overseas at a military base abroad without intrusive interference by American courts keen to protect their rights under either American or international law? What process must the military grant to an American citizen it wishes to hold as an enemy combatant, and is that process different if the citizen is detained domestically by law enforcement, rather than overseas by the military? Must such a person be granted immediate access to a lawyer or can he be held incommunicado for intelligence-gathering purposes? And if he can be so detained, for how long? The answers to these questions are only a little clearer today than they were a few months ago. The Court has only begun to forge the regime that, in the absence of congressional intervention, will govern the detention of enemy combatants. Until that regime comes into clearer focus, it will be too early to determine the real winners and losers in this landmark struggle.

It is not, however, too early to begin assessing the performance of the responsible institutions of American government and civil society with respect to the forging of this regime—that is, to look seriously at the engagement so far among the courts, the administration, Congress, and the civil liberties and human rights groups that have opposed the administration's policies. The exercise, in my judgment, flatters none of the aforementioned institutions. Congress has simply abandoned the field, leaving a series of questions, which obviously require legislative solutions, to a dialogue between the executive and judicial branches. The administration has encouraged this abdication by, instead of seeking legislative input, consistently asserting the most needlessly extreme vision of executive power to resolve novel problems unilaterally. By doing so, it has all but guaranteed a skeptical reception for even its stronger arguments. The courts, meanwhile, have proven uneven in the extreme both at the lower court level and at the Supreme Court. For their part, the human rights and civil liberties communities have responded to the cases with an almost total lack of pragmatism, advancing a reading of federal and international law no less selective and convenient than the administration's own and consistently failing, over the three years since these cases arose, to offer a plausible alternative to the administration's proposed regime.

Writing in the august company of a storied former appellate judge, a former solicitor general of the United States, and noted law professors and experts on the laws of war and executive power, I will be the first to confess myself outclassed in this volume where debating the relevant doctrines is concerned. Neither actually having been to law school nor remotely possessing the appropriate accent for the role, I cannot even claim to be a mere country lawyer—a status that entitles one to surprise a jury and opposing counsel with one's actual sophistication. What I can claim, being a journalist who has covered these cases almost since the day they were filed, is a unique vantage point on the way they developed and the institutional failures that caused them to develop as they did. Throughout the cases' histories, I have spoken at length with officials of all three branches. I have watched as different individuals within those branches struggled— often in vain—to point their institutions in more constructive directions,[7] and I have been in frequent communication with counsel for the detainees. I have, as a consequence, an unusually comprehensive view of the cases.

In the end, the enemy combatant cases—at least so far—stand as a kind of case study of the consequence of abandoning to the adversarial litigation system a sensitive policy debate in which powerful and legitimate constitutional concerns animate both sides. By nearly universal agreement, these cases were submitted to common-law decision making in the face of almost-as-universal agreement that the extant body of law did not fully address the novel conditions of the war on terrorism. As a result, as I shall attempt to show, nuance was lost, flexibility and imagination in envisioning an appropriate

7. I detail some of the struggle within the Justice Department, for example, in Benjamin Wittes, "Enemy Americans," *The Atlantic Monthly*, July/August 2004, 127.

regime were jettisoned, and the courts were left to split the difference between polar arguments to which few Americans would actually sign on and which should not have defined the terms of the discussion. It needn't have been this way. But until Congress assumes responsibility for crafting a system to handle enemy combatants, the regime necessarily will remain a crude, judge-made hybrid of the criminal and military law traditions that will, I suspect, satisfy nobody save the judges who—piece by piece, bit by bit, question by question—will decree it into existence.

II.

It overstates the matter to say that the enemy combatant cases were full of sound and fury and signifying nothing, but they certainly signified a great deal less than their sound and fury portended. It is worth, therefore, beginning by examining exactly what the Court did, what it didn't do, and what questions it left unaddressed.

To begin with the least consequential case, in *Rumsfeld v. Padilla*, the Court did virtually nothing at all—clarifying only that a habeas petitioner in military custody must bring suit in a court with jurisdiction over his immediate physical custodian.[8] Although this holding was in considerable tension with the Court's ruling concerning Guantanamo—where it divined jurisdiction for seemingly any federal court in the country—it was neither especially surprising nor substantively important. It affects, after all, not one jot the procedural rights an accused enemy combatant will enjoy, nor does it alter at all the substantive standard the government must satisfy in order to justify the combatant's detention. It affects only the question of what court he must appear in to challenge that detention.

The only feature of *Padilla* that seems important at all is a footnote in the dissent, in which four members of the Court appear to

8. *Rumsfeld v. Padilla*, 124 S. Ct. 2711 (2004).

address the case's merits head on and dismiss the government's substantive position that President Bush could, under current authorities, designate Jose Padilla—a citizen suspected of planning terrorist attacks on al Qaeda's behalf—as an enemy combatant and hold him as such. "Consistent with the judgment of the Court of Appeals," wrote Justice John Paul Stevens, "I believe that the Non-Detention Act, 18 U.S.C. § 4001(a), prohibits—and the Authorization for Use of Military Force Joint Resolution, 115 Stat. 224, adopted on September 18, 2001, does not authorize—the protracted, incommunicado detention of American citizens arrested in the United States."[9] This language, though certainly dicta, suggests that a majority on the Court may exist for the proposition that someone in Padilla's position, a suspected al Qaeda operative arrested domestically, must either be charged criminally and prosecuted or else released—at least in the absence of a more explicit congressional authorization for enemy combatant detentions. Justice Antonin Scalia wrote in dissent in *Hamdi* that he did not believe a citizen could be detained as an enemy combatant at all, an opinion Justice Stevens joined.[10] Combine the two opinions, and you may have a glimmering of the Court's future direction on this question. So far, however, *Padilla* stands for nothing but a perfectly pedestrian jurisdictional point: that an enemy combatant detained domestically has to go to his local federal court for relief. Which court should hear the claims of detainees was hardly the question that animated the spirited public discussion of enemy combatants over the past three years. So clearly, *Padilla* answers nothing.

The Court said a lot more in *Hamdi*, and in important respects it did repudiate the military's position. The government, after all, had argued that the courts should show nearly total deference to the executive branch's determinations concerning citizens alleged to be

9. *Id.* n. 8 at 2735.
10. *Hamdi*, 124 S. Ct. at 2660.

enemy combatants: They should rely entirely on the government's factual allegations, as laid out in a hearsay affidavit by a midlevel Defense Department official. The detainee need not have any ability to contest these allegations or any assistance of counsel in challenging his detention. And the standard of review itself should be trivial, merely whether the material in the cursory, page-and-a-half affidavit would, if presumed true, support the designation. Eight members of the Court rejected each of these suggestions. The controlling plurality opinion insisted that Yaser Esam Hamdi had a right to contest his designation and to submit evidence to the court in doing so, that he had a right to the assistance of counsel, and, it insisted, that the government's designation be supported with "credible evidence."[11] Rivkin's and Casey's contention that the decision was really a victory is belied by the fact that the plurality opinion in *Hamdi* tracks closely with — indeed, in critical respects, is less favorable to the government than — the district court's opinion in *Padilla*, an opinion the government aggressively appealed.

But if *Hamdi* establishes that the executive's hand is not entirely free, it by no means clarifies that judicial review — even in cases involving citizens — will function as a meaningful, as opposed to a symbolic, restraint on executive behavior. For starters, the government won on a truly fundamental point in the case: The plurality reaffirmed the power in principle of the president to detain a citizen as an enemy combatant — a power it articulated in *Ex parte Quirin* — writing that "[t]here is no bar to this Nation's holding one of its own citizens as an enemy combatant."[12] In other words, the plurality allowed the military to exempt an individual from the full protections of criminal process on the basis of a finding that he has enlisted in a foreign military struggle against the United States in the context of a use of force authorized by Congress. The Court's acceptance of this basic premise of the government's argument is no small matter.

11. *Id.* at 2649.
12. *Id.* at 2640.

Moreover, Justice Sandra Day O'Connor was a bit cagey on the subject of Hamdi's access to counsel, and what she doesn't hold is as important as what she does. "Hamdi asks us to hold that the Fourth Circuit also erred by denying him immediate access to counsel upon his detention and by disposing of the case without permitting him to meet with an attorney," she noted at the end of the plurality opinion. "Since our grant of certiorari in this case, Hamdi has been appointed counsel, with whom he has met for consultation purposes on several occasions, and with whom he is now being granted unmonitored meetings. He unquestionably has the right to access to counsel *in connection with the proceedings on remand.* No further consideration of this issue is necessary at this stage of the case"[13] (emphasis added). The language granting Hamdi access to counsel is ringing. It is framed in the language of constitutional rights, not—as the district courts in both *Hamdi* and *Padilla* envisioned it—as a discretionary grant of access for the purpose of airing all the issues in the case fully. But as the italicized language indicates, the "right" is only clear prospectively. Justice O'Connor did not address the question of whether Hamdi had this right from the outset of the litigation, when the right attached, or whether it was appropriate for the government—in the interests of interrogating him for intelligence—to have withheld it for two years.

What's more, Justice O'Connor left open the possibility that her due process concerns could be satisfied by tribunals within the military and that had such military process been available to Hamdi, judicial review would have been far more deferential as a consequence. "Plainly, the 'process' Hamdi has received is not that to which he is entitled under the Due Process Clause," she wrote. But "[t]here remains the possibility that the standards we have articulated could be met by an appropriately authorized and properly constituted military tribunal. Indeed, it is notable that military regulations already

13. *Id.* at 2652.

provide for such process in related instances, dictating that tribunals be made available to determine the status of enemy detainees who assert prisoner-of-war status under the Geneva Convention. . . . In the absence of such process, however, a court that receives a petition for a writ of habeas corpus from an alleged enemy combatant must itself ensure that the minimum requirements of due process are achieved."[14] The tribunals to which she refers are, historically speaking, cursory affairs that do not involve a right to counsel or contemplate a great deal of factual development. If the import of *Hamdi* is that the military can, in the future, buy the total judicial deference it sought in this case by affording citizens alleged to be enemy combatants the limited process contemplated by Article 5 of the Third Geneva Convention, then the military has lost little and gained much in its apparent defeat this time around.

In short, although the government was rebuked by the Court, it is by no means clear that the next time an American citizen is captured abroad while apparently fighting for the other side, the military will not be able to behave very nearly as it behaved toward Hamdi — that is, hold him incommunicado for an extended period of time while interrogating him for intelligence. Nor are we likely to find out the answer to this question any time soon. The *Hamdi* case, after all, has been settled, and Hamdi himself released. Although clarity could come as a consequence of future developments in *Padilla*, there is a substantial possibility that it too will become moot, not because of Padilla's release but because of his criminal indictment.[15] The ques-

---

14. *Id.* at 2651.

15. Padilla's habeas case was refiled in South Carolina in light of the Supreme Court's ruling and was argued in federal district court there early in 2005. U.S. District Judge Henry F. Floyd, on February 28, 2005, found in favor of Padilla and issued a writ of habeas corpus. The government immediately announced plans to appeal. Even as the habeas case has progressed, however, there has been some indication that Padilla is now a cooperating witness in a case unrelated to the circumstances of his arrest, a status that implies that a plea may be in the works. See Dan Christensen and Vanessa Blum, "Padilla Implicated in Florida Terror Case," *Legal Times*, September 20, 2004, p. 18.

tion of whether enemy combatant detention is a legally tenable approach for the government toward citizens remains, despite the cases, very much an open one.

The high court's pronouncements with respect to the detainees at Guantanamo Bay, Cuba, were just as Delphic. The justices, by a 6–3 vote, declared that the federal courts had jurisdiction to consider habeas petitions filed on behalf of inmates at the facility. Indeed, the justices formulated the question posed by the case in language emphasizing the stakes for liberty and the rule of law: "What is presently at stake is only whether the federal courts have jurisdiction to determine the legality of the Executive's potentially indefinite detention of individuals who claim to be wholly innocent of wrongdoing," Justice Stevens wrote.[16] The assertion of jurisdiction necessarily cast the Bush administration's conduct in a negative light, implying that there were substantial questions to litigate concerning the legality of the detentions—questions that rendered the Court's jurisdiction significant. And, to be sure, Justice Stevens's language did nothing to dispel this impression. He noted at one point in a footnote, for example, that "Petitioners' allegations—that, although they have engaged neither in combat nor in acts of terrorism against the United States, they have been held in Executive detention for more than two years in territory subject to the long-term, exclusive jurisdiction and control of the United States, without access to counsel and without being charged with any wrongdoing—unquestionably describe 'custody in violation of the Constitution or laws or treaties of the United States.'"[17]

Heartless as it may sound, however, this apparently unobjectionable statement may not actually be true. That is to say, even if all of the Guantanamo inmates were completely innocent of any wrongdoing—which they most assuredly are not—and, more important,

16. *Rasul*, 124 S. Ct. at 2699.
17. *Id.* n. 15 at 2698.

even were they all demonstrably not combatants, it would remain something of a puzzle what, if any, judicially enforceable law would be implicated by such reckless executive behavior. Indeed, the court has not generally held that the protections of the Bill of Rights apply to aliens overseas.[18] The Geneva Conventions have not traditionally been regarded as self-executing, and Congress has never explicitly given the courts power to enforce the terms of the conventions, which have been generally guaranteed by diplomatic pressures and reciprocity, not by litigation.[19] Exactly what does American law promise a suspected Taliban soldier—much less an al Qaeda operative—that a court in this country can ensure he gets?

Since only the jurisdictional question was before it, the Court avowedly declined to answer this question. "Whether and what further proceedings may become necessary after respondents make their response to the merits of petitioners' claims are matters that we need

18. See, e.g., *U.S. v. Verdugo-Urquidez*, 494 U.S. 259 (1990), and *Johnson v. Eisentrager*, 339 U.S. 763, 784 (1950). Although the latter decision has been called into question by *Rasul*, the former has not. And there still exists no authority for the proposition that the Bill of Rights limits government action against aliens operating in foreign theaters of warfare. The Court, however, has applied the Bill of Rights to some degree in American territories overseas. So, in the wake of *Rasul*, the Court will have to decide whether Guantanamo is truly foreign territory or whether it is analogous to such overseas possessions.

19. In the wake of *Rasul*, this premise has come into considerable doubt. In *Hamdi v. Rumsfeld* (D.D.C. 04-CV-1519, Nov. 8, 2004), U.S. District Judge James Robertson held that the Third Geneva Convention was self-executing. See, in particular, pages 25–26. "Because the Geneva Conventions were written to protect individuals, because the Executive Branch of our government implemented the Geneva Conventions for fifty years without questioning the absence of implementing legislation, because Congress clearly understood that the Conventions did not require implementing legislation except in a few specific areas, and because nothing in the Third Geneva Convention itself manifests the contracting parties' intention that it become effective as domestic law without the enactment of implementing legislation, I conclude that, insofar as it is pertinent here, the Third Geneva Convention is a self-executing treaty." The opinion, under appeal as of this writing, can be found at http://www.dcd.uscourts.gov/04-1519.pdf. See also *In re Guantanamo Detainee Cases* (D.D.C. 02-CV-0299, Jan. 31, 2005), pages 70–71, which can be found at http://www.dcd.uscourts.gov/02-299b.pdf.

not address now," Justice Stevens wrote.[20] And this coyness can, I suppose, be reasonably defended as judicial restraint—an unwillingness to address questions before they are fully presented and briefed. But the result is that nobody knows today what the great rebuke to the executive branch that the Court delivered in *Rasul* means in practice. Detainees have filed numerous claims since the decisions, alleging treaty, statutory, and constitutional deprivations. The great rebuke could be a giant nothing. If the Court has, in fact, asserted jurisdiction in order to determine later that no judicially cognizable rights have been violated, the executive will have lost nothing save a certain embarrassment and the inconvenience of having to brief and argue the subsequent legal questions.[21] Civil libertarians and human rights groups—not to mention the detainees—will have won nothing more than the satisfaction of having lost on the merits, rather than on a jurisdictional point. The litigation will have rendered the executive branch barely more accountable than had it won on the jurisdictional point—indeed, the administration will have had its legal position actively *affirmed*, not just deemed unreviewable. The detainees will certainly be no freer as a consequence of their victory. On the other hand, if the Court is truly prepared to act as the enforcer of legal rights toward alien detainees who have never set foot in this country, *Rasul* heralds a sea change in judicial power in wartime, an

---

20. *Id.* at 2699.

21. The first of the rash of detainee suits to follow *Rasul* played out in exactly this fashion at the district court level. In *Khalid v. Bush* (D.D.C. CV 04-1142, Jan. 19, 2005), U.S. District Judge Richard Leon held that notwithstanding *Rasul*, "no viable legal theory exists by which [a federal court] could issue a writ of habeas corpus under these circumstances." The decision can be found at http://www.dcd .uscourts.gov/04-1142.pdf. On the other hand, less than two weeks later, Senior Judge Joyce Hens Green of the same court handed down *In re Guantanamo Detainee Cases*, in which she held precisely the opposite: The Fifth Amendment applies in Guantanamo and confers due process rights that are violated by the government's review procedures, and the Geneva Conventions are self-executing and confer individual litigable rights as well.

earthquake of untold magnitude and importance. The Court could also attempt some kind of intermediate step.

But the fog does not even end there. For the Court was less than clear about precisely what it was holding, even with respect to mere jurisdiction. At times, the majority opinion seemed to depend on the unique legal status of Guantanamo Bay, which is leased on an indefinite basis to the United States and subject during that time to the "exclusive jurisdiction and control" of the United States.[22] At other times, however, the decision appears to rest on no such gimmick, relying instead only on the allegation of an illegal detention and the Court's proper jurisdiction over the Pentagon: "Petitioners contend that they are being held in federal custody in violation of the laws of the United States. No party questions the District Court's jurisdiction over petitioners' custodians. . . . [The habeas statute], by its terms, requires nothing more."[23] So although it is clear, after the court's decision, that the federal courts have the power to decide legal questions concerning the Guantanamo detainees, it is no clearer than before that decision whether the detentions at Guantanamo are in fact legally defective, nor is it clear whether the executive could still evade federal court oversight altogether by simply avoiding detention facilities abroad that happen to be formally leased to exclusive, indefinite American jurisdiction. Once again, the Court left all of the fundamental questions unanswered.

In short, although it is indisputable that the administration suffered a major atmospheric defeat at the hands of solid, though shifting, majorities of the Court, it remains premature to describe the true winners and losers in the cases. One cannot, at this stage, say—with Rivkin and Casey—that the administration has won the fight. But one has to acknowledge the possibility that the doctrinal seeds of its ultimate victory are germinating in the Court's decisions, and one

22. *Rasul*, 124 S. Ct. at 2693.
23. *Id.* at 2698.

cannot dismiss the possibility that, in the long run, the true import of the decisions will lie more in what they permit than in what they forbid.

III.

Even in this moment of uncertainty as to the ultimate significance of the cases, however, one can attempt to assess the performance of the institutions, governmental and other, that have brought us to this point. The one that has attracted the most attention—criticism, controversy, and defense—is the executive branch. This is natural enough given the president's necessary leadership role in moments of national crisis, his control over the military, and, in this instance, his personal responsibility for many of the policies in question. Padilla was, after all, plucked out of the criminal justice system on the personal order of President Bush. It is right and proper that President Bush should be held accountable for the detention policies practiced by his administration. Still, in my judgment, the centrality of executive branch decisions in the public discussion of detention policies seems slightly too forgiving of the failures of other institutions. What's more, the criticism seems, in a fundamental sense, misdirected. For the president's original sin lay not simply—or even chiefly—in the substance of the positions he took with respect to captured enemy fighters. It lay, rather, in his utter unwillingness to seek legal sanction from Congress for those positions.

When you step back and examine the detention policies of the war on terrorism from the highest altitude, the administration's posture is not quite as outrageous as it seems from the ground. After all, countries at war detain the enemy. They interrogate those captured enemy fighters not entitled to privileged treatment. They don't usually provide foreign fighters with lawyers, except when those fighters are tried for war crimes. And they claim the right to hold those fighters until hostilities end. In the broadest sense, therefore, there is nothing exceptional about the Bush administration's position toward those it has detained. What's more, the civil liberties intrusion of these policies is quite constrained compared with past wars. The affected universe of detainees is limited to those the military believes to be fighters for the other side—neither large civilian populations (like the Japanese Americans interned during World War II) nor opponents of the war (like socialists during World War I). And in contrast to the Civil War, the writ of habeas corpus has not been suspended, so the courts remain at least formally open for business in judging any challenges to detentions. There is, quite simply, nothing intrinsically unreasonable about the administration's desire to use the traditional presidential wartime power to detain enemy combatants in this particular conflict.

What is unreasonable, however, is the pretense, almost since the beginning of the conflict, that the proper altitude for considering this problem is that of a jetliner. For zoom in only a little, and the differences between this conflict and those that have preceded it make the clean application of prior law and precedent nearly impossible. What does it mean to detain combatants for the duration of hostilities in a conflict that may never end? In a conflict with a shadowy, international, nonhierarchical, nonstate actor as enemy, what would victory look like if we achieved it? If we then released detainees, as international law requires, wouldn't that act merely restart the conflict? More immediately, given that al Qaeda does not fight along a front but seeks to infiltrate American society and destroy it from within, how can one reliably distinguish between combatants and mere sympathizers or even uninvolved parties caught in the wrong place at the wrong time? These differences are not mere oddities of the current conflict. They are fundamental challenges to the legal regime that governs traditional warfare, which presupposes clearly defined armies and a moment of negotiated peace, after which those captured will be repatriated as a consequence of diplomatic negotiation. The premise of detention in traditional warfare is that the warring parties have no issue with the individual soldier detained, who is presumed to be honorable. That premise is simply false in the current war, in which America's battle is very much with the individual jihadist. After all, unlike, say, Germany or Japan, al Qaeda is nothing more than the sum of its members.

Given the profound differences between the war on terror and past conflicts, there was no good reason for the administration to treat the resolution of questions as simple matters of executive discretion. They are essentially legislative in character—for notwithstanding the administration's pretenses, they go far beyond questions of how to apply old law to new circumstances. Rather, they represent the questions that will define the legal regime we, as a society, create in order to govern a situation never fully imagined, let alone encountered, in the past. As such, it was sheer folly for the Bush administration to attempt to answer them on its own—and that folly was as profoundly self-destructive as it was injurious to liberty and fairness.

The simple truth is that the administration could have gotten almost anything it wanted from Congress in the way of detention authority for enemy aliens abroad in the wake of September 11. If the debate over the USA Patriot Act proved anything, it was that Congress had little appetite for standing in the way of the most robust response the executive could muster. The administration would likely have had to stomach a certain amount of process for the detainees, particularly for citizens held domestically. One can imagine that Congress might have required some eventual provision of counsel for some detainees, perhaps even mandated a forum in which the evidence against them in some form could be tested. The administration may even have been forced to provide the process contemplated by Article 5 of the Third Geneva Convention for distinguishing between lawful and unlawful combatants—a process it certainly should have been granting in any event. In my estimation, however, it is simply inconceivable that Congress would have crafted a regime that did not amply accommodate the president's wartime needs, particularly if

President Bush had been clear about what he needed, why he needed it, and what the stakes were if he didn't get it. Going to Congress would have required two things of President Bush: a willingness to accept certain minimal limits on executive conduct imposed from the outside and, more fundamentally, a recognition that the wartime powers of the president, while vast, are not plenary—an acceptance that the presidential power to wage war can be enhanced by acknowledging the legislature's role in legitimizing it. Had Bush proceeded thus—as presidents often have in past conflicts—he would have entered his court battles with clear statutory warrant for his positions. Had this happened, I believe the deference he sought from the Supreme Court would have been forthcoming and very nearly absolute.

But Bush did not take this approach. His administration's insistence on what might be termed Article II fundamentalism caused him to take maximalist positions that are genuinely troubling: The president's judgment that a person is an enemy combatant is essentially unreviewable. The courts should defer to the executive, even in the absence of an administrative record to which to defer. Long-term detentions without trials of hundreds of people are entirely outside the purview of the courts. They all amount to the same basic position: Trust us. Trust the executive branch, in a wholly new geopolitical environment, acting with the barest and most general approval from the other political branch, to generate an entirely new legal system with the power of freedom and liberty and life and death over anyone it says belongs in that system. The executive branch learned last spring that exactly one member of the Supreme Court—Clarence Thomas—trusts President Bush that much. The court's skepticism seems to me to have been an entirely foreseeable result that competent counsel advising the president ought to have hedged against. When the history of this period is written, I feel confident that Bush will be deemed exceedingly ill-served by his top legal advisers.

IV.

But the president's responsibility, however heavy, is not exclusive. Congress, after all, has its own independent duty to legislate in response to problems that arise in the course of the nation's life. And in a system of separated powers, Congress is not meant to legislate simply for the executive's convenience or at its beck and call. Indeed, if the executive branch sought to shunt the legislature aside in this episode, the legislature certainly proved itself a most willing shuntee. Congress institutionally seemed more than content to sideline itself and let the executive branch and the courts sort out what the law should be.

This abandonment of the field is disturbing on several levels. At the most analytical, America's constitutional design presupposes that each branch of government will assert its powers, that those powers will clash, and that this clash will prevent the accumulation of power in any one branch. This is the famous premise of Federalist 51: "[T]he great security against a gradual concentration of the several powers in the same department, consists in giving to those who administer each department the necessary constitutional means and personal motives to resist encroachments of the others. The provision for defense must in this, as in all other cases, be made commensurate to the danger of attack. Ambition must be made to counteract ambition." Yet in the war on terrorism, Congress has done very nearly the opposite of countering the executive's ambition. It has run from its own powers on questions on which its assertion of rightful authority would be helpful, and it sloughed the difficult choices onto the two branches of government less capable than itself of designing new systems for novel problems.

The problem of congressional abdication of its responsibilities during wartime is not exactly new. It is most remarked upon in the context of the decision to go to war in the first place, which migrated in the twentieth century almost entirely to the executive branch. John

Hart Ely noted, "It is common to style this shift a usurpation, but that oversimplifies to the point of misstatement. It's true our Cold War presidents generally wanted it that way, but Congress (and the courts) ceded the ground without a fight. In fact . . . the legislative surrender was a self-interested one: Accountability is pretty frightening stuff."[24] Ely's remedy for this problem—treating war powers as presenting justiciable questions with which the courts should be actively engaged—presents substantial difficulties on its own terms. Judges, after all, are not foreign policy experts, and decisions concerning war and peace are quintessentially political judgments, not principled legal ones. But even a robustly activist judiciary that was eager to explore such uncharted territories would have difficulty designing an appropriate regime for enemy combatants, because, to put it bluntly, the terms of any debate presented by litigation are destined to be too narrow.

Having no legislative involvement quite simply cuts off policy options. Once you consider the problem of enemy combatant detentions as a set of policy questions, a world of options opens. This world necessarily remains elusive to those who insist on finding in the doctrinal space between *Ex parte Milligan*[25] and *Ex parte Quirin* the answer to the question of how a Louisiana-born Saudi picked up in Afghanistan must be treated in a world in which a hegemonic United States has to consider nuclear terrorism a possibility. To cite only one conceivable example, the Constitution allows the civil commitment of mentally ill citizens who pose a danger to themselves or others. For a reasonably imaginative Congress, this might be a far better model for the alleged al Qaeda operative captured domestically than either the traditional laws of war or the criminal justice apparatus. A regime of civil commitment, after all, would recognize the preventive nature of the arrest, and it would co-opt the use of a process that

24. John Hart Ely, *War and Responsibility: Constitutional Lessons of Vietnam and Its Aftermath* (Princeton, N.J.: Princeton University Press, 1993), ix.
25. *Ex parte Milligan*, 71 U.S. 2 (1866).

American society already tolerates as adequate for indefinite detentions in another context. Surely, al Qaeda operatives pose at least as
great a threat to society as do schizophrenics.

One can imagine other models as well. Immigration law tolerates long detentions based almost entirely on executive branch process. Various forms of military tribunals might be attractive as well, as
Hamdi intimates. The point is that the terms of the debate are today
artificially constrained by the unwillingness of the one branch with
the capacity to imagine a system from scratch to engage the problem
at all. Although individual members of Congress have raised the
issue,[26] the congressional leadership—perhaps out of an unwillingness to publicly second-guess the Bush administration, perhaps out
of sheer laziness, most likely out of a combination of the two—has
shown no interest in actually legislating. Congress, in short, has concurred in the executive's unilateralism, offering neither legal support
for its positions nor redirection of them. By the consent of both political branches, in other words, the design of the detention regime is
being determined in a dialogue between the president and the courts.

Perhaps the most peculiar aspect of this decision is that it sparked
so little controversy. The fact that few observers even comment upon
Congress's absence from the discussion says a great deal about how
Americans have come intuitively to weigh the responsibilities and
contributions of the three branches of government. To be sure, many
critics of the administration complain of the absence of specific congressional authority for detentions or military commissions by way of
arguing against the legality of the administration's course. But the
critics, by and large, are not urging congressional intervention, much
less are they describing what a constructive intervention would look
like. They have merely cited its absence as a bar to whatever action
the administration proposes. Somehow, everyone seems to agree that

---

26. See, e.g., House Resolution 1029, the Detention of Enemy Combatants Act,
introduced by Rep. Adam Schiff (D-CA) on February 23, 2003.

the initial crack at writing the rules should be left to common-law jurisprudence.

V.

This agreement—which remains, frankly, inexplicable to me—has put a considerable premium on the performance of a nongovernmental actor: the human rights and civil liberties groups that opposed the military in these litigations. Although Padilla, Hamdi, and the Guantanamo plaintiffs all had counsel to argue their cases, these groups greatly magnified the arguments against the administration's course, both in amicus filings and in the broader realm of public debate. Consequently, they became, in some sense, the "other side" of the debate—the organized force whose arguments marked the major alternative to the direction the administration chose. Unfortunately, they did not provide the Court with a useful alternative to the administration's vision, for their arguments were marked at once by failures of pragmatism and weak and selective understanding of doctrine. This is forgivable in the case of defense lawyers, who are obliged to advance the arguments most likely to aid their individual clients. And in the human rights and civil liberties groups, the decision was undoubtedly as much strategic as it was driven by conviction. By staking out a hard line, the groups ensured that they had not conceded key points even before any compromises took place. But the result of their wholesale adoption of the defense arguments was to present the court with a strategy for preserving liberty that was as unembracable as the administration's strategy for ensuring security.

Doctrinally, the ground staked out by the human rights community made fetishes of certain components of the laws of war and American constitutional law, even while ignoring other countervailing components of the same bodies of law. The human rights groups generally elided the importance of *Ex parte Quirin*, for example, which quite unambiguously endorses the premise that the American citizen can be detained by the military as an unlawful combatant.[27] Though their briefs were usually more careful than to make this error, they often seemed to deny in public statements that a detainee could be held as an unlawful combatant at all—a position flatly at odds with long-standing traditions of warfare. They nearly uniformly denied that the congressional authorization for the use of force against al Qaeda and its state sponsors necessarily implied the lesser power to detain combatants.[28] And all regarded it as self-evident that federal courts should supervise the detentions of noncitizens abroad—something they have never done previously in American history.[29]

One doesn't have to be a raging enthusiast for executive power to worry that these positions, particularly cumulatively, are simply inconsistent with any serious attempt to wage war against al Qaeda— even an attempt that does not partake of the excesses in which the Bush administration so indulged. In the rather fanciful regime the human rights groups appear to contemplate (and I acknowledge here that I am blending different arguments into a mélange that might reflect no single group's precise position), the citizen is entitled to criminal process even if caught on a battlefield. The courts are engaged in day-to-day monitoring of executive compliance with the Geneva Conventions—though those treaties are not self-executing and have not historically been enforced through judicial action. Even the unlawful combatant—that is, a combatant not entitled to the

27. The briefs in *Hamdi* can be found at http://www.jenner.com/news/ news_item.asp?id=12551224. Those in *Padilla* can be found at http://www.jenner .com/news/news_item.asp?id=12539624. The amicus filings of the American Civil Liberties Union, the Center for National Security Studies, Human Rights First, and other human rights and civil liberties groups, for example, all deny that current law authorizes enemy combatant detentions in at least one of the two cases, even if the detainee is granted a meaningful ability to contest his designation.

28. See, again, the amicus filings in both *Hamdi* and *Padilla*. Interestingly, the brief of the libertarian Cato Institute presents a notable exception.

29. The briefs in *Rasul* can be found at http://www.jenner.com/news/ news_item.asp?id=12520724. The range of institutional support for the assertion of jurisdiction is dramatic.

status of prisoner of war—is nonetheless entitled to the same criminal procedure, the court-martial, as both the lawful combatant and the American soldier accused of misconduct. It is a beautiful vision, but it does not happen to be the vision encapsulated in either international law or American law. And it's hard even to imagine fighting a war within its constraints. Should someone like Khalid Sheikh Muhammad be entitled to immediate access to counsel upon capture in Pakistan? Should he be able immediately to file a habeas corpus action alleging deprivations of his constitutional and treaty rights? There is embedded in this vision a very deep discomfort with the premise that the war on terrorism is, legally speaking, a war at all.

The consequence of the human rights groups staking out such unflinching ground was that the courts were faced, in all three cases, with a choice between extremes. Instead of confronting a well-con-structed—or even a badly constructed—statutory scheme that sought to balance the competing constitutional values at stake in these detentions, it confronted a choice between total deference to the executive, aided only by the most general support from Congress, or total rejection of its claims, including its legitimate claims. In other words, it faced a choice between throwing the baby out with the bathwater and drinking the bathwater. The unifying theme of the Supreme Court's action in the enemy combatant cases is the refusal to choose—that is, the insistence on splitting the difference, even where prior precedent gave it scant leeway to do so.

VI.

The performance of the courts in this endeavor was enormously uneven. Unlike the executive, which ultimately takes a unitary position on virtually all issues, and the Congress, which essentially took no position on the enemy combatant questions, the different courts, not to mention the different judges within individual courts, took several positions. And these ran the gamut in terms of quality and seriousness.

For example, the district court that handled Padilla's case in New York produced—notwithstanding its ultimate reversal on the jurisdictional question on which the Supreme Court decided the case—the single most compelling judicial opinion yet written on the due process rights of citizens held as enemy combatants.[30] Chief Judge Michael Mukasey's handling of Padilla's case was a model of the combination of deference and skepticism that judges need to show in the war on terrorism, and it clearly became the model for Justice O'Connor's plurality opinion at the Supreme Court level. Judge Robert Doumar in Virginia, by contrast, was completely out of his depth in *Hamdi*. His rulings served to muddy, not clarify, the issues, as did his petulance toward government counsel.

More particularly for our purposes, in both appellate courts in the domestic cases—in the Fourth Circuit in *Hamdi* and in the Second Circuit in *Padilla*—the majority opinions simply adopted one or the other of the ultimately untenable hard-line positions, either the government's or that of the human rights groups and defense bar. In *Hamdi*, the Fourth Circuit declared the government's submission adequate to consign a citizen to his fate, at least where it is "undisputed" that he was captured in a "zone of active combat operations abroad."[31] To render beyond dispute the question of whether Hamdi was, in fact, captured in a zone of active combat abroad without hearing from Hamdi himself, the court found putative factual concessions in court filings, which the man had never seen or approved and which were written by lawyers with whom he had never been permitted to meet.[32] The Second Circuit, meanwhile, declared Padilla's detention unlawful, buying in its entirety the notion that Congress's authorization to use force had not triggered the traditional war power of detaining the enemy until hostilities were at an end.[33] In

30. *Rumsfeld v. Padilla*, 233 F. Supp. 2d 564 (2002).
31. *Hamdi v. Rumsfeld*, 316 F. 3d 450, 476 (2003).
32. *Id.* at 471, 473, and 474.
33. *Rumsfeld v. Padilla*, 352 F. 3d 695 (2003).

both cases, dissenting judges showed considerably more sophistication, taking approaches that approximated the one the high court
plurality ultimately adopted.[34] But because these were dissents in
both courts of appeals, both *Padilla* and *Hamdi* came before the high
court with stark stakes indeed: One court had held that the appropriate process was no process at all, while the other had held that—
at least absent a neurotically specific act of Congress—nothing short
of full criminal process could satisfy the Constitution.

The Guantanamo case approached the courts with the battle
lines drawn similarly sharply, albeit for a different reason. The
Supreme Court's own opinion in *Johnson v. Eisentrager* left little
room for argument at the lower court level as to the jurisdiction of
the federal courts over habeas petitions from the base. The Court
wrote baldly at that time that "[w]e are cited to no instance where a
court, in this or any other country where the writ [of habeas corpus]
is known, has issued it on behalf of an alien enemy who, at no relevant time and in no stage of his captivity, has been within its territorial jurisdiction. Nothing in the text of the Constitution extends
such a right, nor does anything in our statutes."[35] Any lower court
tempted to assert jurisdiction over the base consequently had a high
bar to clear in terms of binding precedent. In the *Rasul* litigation, no
judge even attempted it. The district court wrote, "Given that under
Eisentrager, writs of habeas corpus are not available to aliens held
outside the sovereign territory of the United States, this Court does
not have jurisdiction to entertain the claims made by Petitioners."[36]
The D.C. Circuit Court of Appeals unanimously affirmed, and not
a single judge voted for en banc review.[37] In other words, when the

---

34. See Judge Motz's dissent from denial of rehearing en banc in *Hamdi*,
reported at 337 F. 3d 335, 368 (2003). See also Judge Wesley's dissent in *Padilla*,
reported at 352 F. 3d 695, 726 (2003).

35. *Eisentrager*, 339 U.S. at 763, 767.

36. *Rasul v. Bush*, 215 F. Supp. 2d 55, 72 (2002).

37. *Al Odah v. United States*, 321 F. 3d 1134 (2003). The decision denying

Court considered the petition for certiorari, the justices were facing—
as a consequence of the fidelity of the lower courts to what *Eisentrager*
plainly said—the prospect of being wholly shut out of the discussion
of enemy combatants held abroad. (It should be noted that an attempt
was made by the Ninth Circuit to assert jurisdiction over the base,
but this was after certiorari had already been granted in *Rasul*.[38] Had
the Court declined to consider *Rasul*, it would likely have had to
jump to settle the conflict between the two circuits that developed as
a result of this decision.)

As can probably be gleaned from these remarks, I am far more
sympathetic to the high court's handling of *Hamdi* than to its resolution of *Rasul*. But critically, I believe the instinct behind both decisions was a similar one: the desire to split the baby between the claims
of liberty and the claims of military necessity.

The plurality opinion in *Hamdi*, with all its vagueness and
uncertainty, seems to me a creditable job of balancing constitutional
values, and one that gets the big picture just about right. It acknowledges, first, the fact that the war on terrorism is not a metaphorical
war like the war on drugs or the war on cancer—that is, it is not a
statement of seriousness of purpose on a policy question but an actual
state of military hostilities authorized by Congress and triggering traditional presidential war powers. Second, it acknowledges that
implicit in Congress's authorization to use force is an authorization
to detain those using force on the other side, even if they are American citizens. For different reasons, Justices Stevens, Scalia, Ginsburg,
and Souter would have refused to recognize even this basic premise.
Finally, the plurality recognizes that a citizen so detained is, by virtue
of his citizenship, differently situated from a foreign national and
entitled to a fair and impartial hearing should he choose to contest
his status. These three basic premises seem to me all correct, whether

---

rehearing en banc is reported at *Al Odah v. United States*, 2003 U.S. App. LEXIS
11166.

38. *Gherebi v. Bush*, 374 F. 3d 727 (2003).

they ultimately work to the government's advantage or to that of the detainees. In the absence of guidance from the legislature, I do not think American society could have expected more from the high court than finding this middle road and taking it.

Finding a middle course was naturally harder in *Rasul*. For jurisdiction, like pregnancy, is not a gray area; it either exists, or it doesn't exist. In this instance, the legal argument for jurisdiction was exceptionally weak. To get around *Eisentrager*, the Court had to argue that the famous holding had effectively been overruled in 1973—at least on the question of statutory jurisdiction in habeas cases—in a decision that does not even mention *Eisentrager*.[39] As noted above, the Court left unclear whether its assertion of jurisdiction applied only to Guantanamo or whether any detainee anywhere has access to American courts. For anyone with a sense of judicial restraint, *Rasul* should properly induce some embarrassment, for it is as dismissive of the Court's own precedent as it is disrespectful of the executive branch's reliance on that precedent in designing its detention policies. As Justice Antonin Scalia put it for the three dissenting justices,

> This is not only a novel holding; it contradicts a half-century-old precedent on which the military undoubtedly relied. The Court's contention that *Eisentrager* was somehow negated by *Braden v. 30th Judicial Circuit Court of Ky.*—a decision that dealt with a different issue and did not so much as mention *Eisentrager*—is implausible in the extreme. This is an irresponsible overturning of settled law in a matter of extreme importance to our forces currently in the field. I would leave it to Congress to change [the habeas statute], and dissent from the Court's unprecedented holding.[40] (internal citations omitted)

But if *Rasul* is an embarrassment, it is one that illuminates the

39. See Justice Stevens's discussion in *Rasul* at 2695 concerning *Braden v. 30th Judicial Circuit Court of Ky.*, 410 U.S. 484. See also Justice Scalia's rebuttal concerning *Braden*'s relevance, which begins at 2703.
40. *Id.* at 2703.

same baby-splitting instinct as the plurality opinion in *Hamdi*. For although the Court could not split the difference between the administration and its critics in this case—the substantive issues not being before it yet—it could preserve its ability to split the difference in the future. The result may be a cheap, cynical opinion, but it is one that keeps the justices in the discussion without promising anything tangible. Its vagueness, I believe, is part of its point—a shot across the executive's bow, warning that if it doesn't get its act together, the Court will force it to do so by divining some cognizable rights, just as it divined its own power to consider the detainees' fates in the first place. If the executive behaves responsibly, by contrast, my guess is that the plaintiffs will find that *Rasul* proves an empty vessel for pushing the military toward greater liberality for detainees. In other words, by finding jurisdiction in *Rasul*, however implausibly, the Court positioned itself to play exactly the role it played in *Hamdi*, though admittedly on what will inevitably prove thinner legal reeds.

The baby-splitting instinct evident in these cases is, I suspect, a vision of the future of the legal war on terrorism in the absence of congressional intervention. The courts have positioned themselves not to impose particular processes but, rather, like figure-skating judges at the Olympics, to hold up signs granting marks to the players as they struggle to carve their own way: This process gets a 5.6; this one is inadequate because it lacks a bit more of this value or has too much of that value at the expense of some other one. Because the court is allergic to simply letting one side win—an instinct which, in and of itself, deserves some sympathy given the exceedingly harsh choices posed by the parties—the result is likely to be ongoing uncertainty, the absence of a legal safe harbor for executive conduct, and a big legal question mark hanging over the fates of all detainees held by the military domestically or abroad.

There is, of course, an alternative: a serious and deliberative legislative process that would design a regime within the confines of the Court's dictates to date—a regime to which the courts could defer in the future and which could define the role they should play going forward. This alternative, however, would require two developments: The administration would have to assume a modicum of humility in its dealings with the other branches of government. The administration's foes, meanwhile, would have to accept that war is a reality, not a metaphor, and that, consequently, not everyone detained in the war on terrorism is going to be rushed in front of a magistrate and encouraged to hire Plato Cacheris or Ramsey Clark to handle an immediate habeas action. At this stage, it's hard to say which necessary precondition for a more constructive approach seems a remoter possibility.

5. "Our Perfect Constitution" Revisited

Mark Tushnet

I. Introduction

In 1981, Henry Monaghan published an essay, "Our Perfect Constitution," that was highly critical of the assumption prevalent among enthusiasts of the Warren Court that everything they believed desirable — particularly with respect to individual rights — could be achieved through proper interpretation of the existing Constitution.[1] Focusing on the then-lively conversation among academic constitutional theorists about constitutional interpretation and substantive due process, Monaghan described the "perfect Constitution" assumption in these terms:

> [P]roperly construed, the constitution guarantees against the political order most equality and autonomy values which the

I would like to thank Marty Lederman, Christina Rodriguez, Louis Michael Seidman, and participants in the New York University Law School Faculty Research Workshop for their comments on an earlier version of this chapter.

1. Henry P. Monaghan, *Our Perfect Constitution*, 56 N.Y.U. L. Rev. 353 (1981).

commentators think a twentieth century Western liberal democratic government ought to guarantee to its citizens.[2]

He continued, "Each [commentator] asserts that there is a clear and
substantial connection between the constitution and *current* concep-
tions of political morality, a linkage *not* exhausted by any assumed
constitutional guarantee of a fair political system."[3] As these statements indicate, the "perfect Constitution" assumption is closely tied
to issues of constitutional interpretation.[4]

Monaghan's concluding comments show that his critique actually bites much more deeply, raising questions about the utility of
constitutional interpretation no matter what one's interpretive
approach is. After criticizing the "perfect Constitution" assumption,
Monaghan wrote, "The constitution established a framework of government suitable to meet the middle distance needs of the nation at
the end of the eighteenth century and, with the Civil War amendments, the nation's needs at the turn of the twentieth century."[5] If
that is so, we can describe the "perfect Constitution" assumption differently: The "perfect Constitution" assumption is that the existing
Constitution—properly construed, as Monaghan said—is entirely adequate to meet the perceived needs of contemporary society. Properly
construed, the Constitution authorizes the national government to
engage in all the activities we (the people engaged in the discussion)
believe are necessary to accomplish the goals set out in the Pream-
ble—which is, in the present context, to "insure domestic Tranquility,
provide for the common defence, [and] promote the general Wel-

2. *Id.* at 358 (emphasis in original removed).
3. *Id.*
4. Monaghan's criticism of the commentators he discussed was predicated on
his commitment to an interpretive method centering on originalism tempered by
stare decisis. See, e.g., *id.* at 360 ("I write from the perhaps 'puerile' bias that original
intent is the proper mode of ascertaining constitutional meaning, although important
concessions must now be made to the claims of stare decisis." [citation omitted]. See
also *id.* at 374–83 (defending originalist interpretation against criticisms).
5. *Id.* at 395.

fare." And, properly construed, the Constitution places limits on the exercise of the national government's powers so as to "secure the Blessings of Liberty to ourselves and our Posterity."

The "perfect Constitution" assumption induces people—lawyers and judges in particular—to believe more than that the existing Constitution provides *some* answer to whatever problems we face. The "perfect Constitution" assumption is that the answers we get from the existing Constitution are pretty good ones, though perhaps not the best imaginable ones. So, for example, the existing Constitution justifies the adoption of policies as part of the war on terrorism that effectively combat terrorism without unduly impairing civil liberties.

I argue that the "perfect Constitution" assumption is nearly inescapable. Every justice who wrote an opinion in *Hamdi v. Rumsfeld* made that assumption.[6] This first part of the chapter demonstrates that proposition. In Part II, I explain why the assumption is so prevalent. The circumstances under which constitutional cases arise place real pressure on litigators and judges to assume that the (existing) Constitution provides the resources to solve the problems they face. Failing to find those resources in the existing Constitution means that problems whose solution seems urgent will go unsolved. Yet, it often turns out that the appearance of urgency is unjustified. What seemed at first like an incredibly urgent problem turns out to be a long-term condition. Rather than trying to solve the problem at once, we might as well have taken a breath and tried to resolve the condition at a more leisurely pace.

This process, flowing (as I argue) from the "perfect Constitution" assumption, has generally bad consequences, which I describe in Part III. To preview my conclusion: Although the assumption has some

---

6. *Hamdi v. Rumsfeld*, 124 S. Ct. 2633 (2004). Justice Scalia's endorsement of the assumption came with a modest qualification. *See* text accompanying notes *infra* notes 46–47. For another exemplification of the "perfect Constitution," see Michael Stokes Paulsen, *The Constitution of Necessity*, 79 NOTRE DAME L. REV. 1257 (2004), discussed text accompanying notes 76–83 *infra*.

positive consequences, it forces constitutional development into the mode of interpretation, which is technical and legalistic, rather than into the mode of public constitutional deliberation as exemplified by the possibility of express amendment. As Monaghan suggested, from an originalist point of view, it would be a miracle were the Constitution entirely adequate to address the nation's problems in the twenty-first century.[7] Yet, the same point could be made about a Constitution interpreted by *any* method. The "perfect Constitution" assumption is that, properly construed, the Constitution lets us do whatever we think needs to be done but stops us from doing whatever we should not do. From the standpoint of any single decision maker, however, a Constitution is hardly needed to accomplish that. Such a decision maker *will* do whatever she thinks needs to be done and will *not* do whatever she thinks she should not do. The standard move at this point is one of institutional allocation: The Constitution, properly construed, confers adequate power on the national government's political branches to do what actually needs to be done, and—again, properly construed—it authorizes the courts to ensure that the political branches do not do what should not be done. Constitutional interpretation by the courts thus becomes the key to ensuring that the perfect Constitution operates as it should.[8]

In doing so, it opens the courts to justified criticism of the sort that Monaghan leveled against the Warren Court, and perhaps worse for those of us who do not believe that courts should enjoy any general immunity from criticism, it reduces the role ordinary citizens play in constitutional development.[9] In short, it would be better were

7. But *cf.* CATHERINE DRINKER BOWEN, MIRACLE AT PHILADELPHIA: THE STORY OF THE CONSTITUTIONAL CONVENTION, MAY TO SEPTEMBER 1787 (1966).

8. The institutional allocation poses its own difficulties, to the extent that it appears to license the courts to decide (1) whether the national government's political branches, taken together, have adequate power and, perhaps more important, (2) how the Constitution allocates power among the political branches. For additional discussion, see discussion of Justice Scalia's opinion and the separation of powers aspects of Justice O'Connor's opinion later in this chapter.

9. "Citizens" is a word not without significance in the present context.

the problems that terrorism poses for our constitutional order addressed by the citizenry in general, through constitutional deliberation channeled into the amendment process, rather than exclusively by the courts.[10] The assumption that our Constitution is perfect converts that conceptual possibility into a practical impossibility.

II. The "Perfect Constitution" Assumption in *Hamdi*

Justice O'Connor's plurality opinion clearly displays the "perfect Constitution" assumption in the care with which she constructs the defense of the proposition that the president had the authority to detain Hamdi and in the sloppiness with which she constructs the proposition that the government can continue to hold Hamdi only if it provides him with the opportunity to contest the grounds of his detention in a proceeding with characteristics that Justice O'Connor enumerates. The latter holding attracted the greatest share of public comment, perhaps because it contained the (I assume, deliberately inserted) attention-getting observation that "a state of war is not a blank check for the President when it comes to the rights of the Nation's citizens."[11] The "perfect Constitution" assumption is completely obvious in the plurality's discussion of its holding about due process. The assumption is a bit harder to see in its discussion of presidential power, which is why I begin by bringing out the way in which that discussion makes the "perfect Constitution" assumption.

Justice O'Connor's argument supporting the conclusion that the president had the authority to order Hamdi's detention is constructed

10. I refer to the amendment process primarily for heuristic purposes—that is, to raise the possibility that modes of constitutional deliberation that are more open and public than constitutional litigation would produce better, that is, more stable and defensible, procedures for dealing with the kinds of issues posed by the war on terrorism. Relying on the amendment process as *the* formal mechanism for addressing those issues would require me to assume, as I do not, that the amendment process is one perfect component in an elsewhere imperfect Constitution.

11. *Hamdi*, 124 S. Ct. at 2650.

segment by segment. In form only a careful construction of the
authority the president had under the congressionally enacted Authorization for the Use of Military Force (AUMF), O'Connor's argument
is committed only to the proposition that the president's authority
exists when *all* the segments are in place; take one away, and the
president *might* lack authority (but perhaps he might have such
authority even in the absence of one or more of the segments).[12]
Justice O'Connor's opinion began by noting two preliminary points.
First, the president claimed that Article II confers authority in him
to detain a citizen as an unlawful combatant. Second, the term
"unlawful combatant" was ill-defined. Justice O'Connor's opinion
confined its holding to persons designated as unlawful combatants
who were "part of or supporting forces hostile to the United States
. . . *in Afghanistan* and who engaged in an armed conflict against
the United States *there*."[13] On the first question, Justice O'Connor's
opinion avoided the president's contention by finding that Congress
had, in fact, authorized Hamdi's detention in the AUMF, which
authorized the president to "use all necessary and appropriate force
against those nations, organizations, or persons he determines
planned, authorized, committed or aided the terrorist attacks" or "harbored such organizations or persons."[14]

12. Justice O'Connor's opinion does not commit those who signed it to any
outcome when one of the segments is missing. Four justices—Scalia, Stevens, Souter,
and Ginsburg—would have held that Hamdi's detention was not within the president's power (the latter two because the detention was not authorized by Congress),
and Justice Breyer joined Justice Stevens's dissenting opinion in *Rumsfeld v. Padilla*,
124 S. Ct. 2711 (2004), which asserted that the detention of an American citizen
who had been seized outside the theater of war was unconstitutional. There would
thus appear to be five justices who think that the president lacks constitutional
authority to order the detention of an American citizen absent congressional authorization or arising from a seizure outside the theater of war.

13. *Hamdi*, 124 S. Ct. at 2639 (emphasis added, internal quotation marks
deleted).

14. Quoted *id.* at 2635. Justice Souter concluded that the AUMF did not authorize the detention of U.S. citizens, and that, in light of another statute's requirement
that "[n]o citizens shall be imprisoned or otherwise detained by the United States

Justice O'Connor's opinion found "no doubt that individuals who fought against the United States in Afghanistan as part of the Taliban" were covered by the AUMF.[15] Relying on the traditional laws of war, the opinion found that detention of such individuals "for the duration of the particular conflict in which they were captured" was a "fundamental and accepted . . . incident to war,"[16] a means of ensuring that opponents would not return to the battlefield. Hamdi argued that Congress had not authorized indefinite detention, to which Justice O'Connor's opinion replied by again invoking the laws of war, which allow detention for as long as "active hostilities" last.[17] Conceding the ambiguity of defining in advance the termination point of a "war on terrorism," the opinion said that it was enough for purposes of Hamdi's case that "[a]ctive combat operations against Taliban fighters apparently are ongoing in Afghanistan." Because the armed conflict giving rise to Hamdi's seizure was continuing, the traditional purpose of detention—to prevent someone from returning to a battlefield—was served by his detention.[18]

---

except pursuant to an Act of Congress," 18 U.S.C. § 4001(a), the president lacked (statutory) authority to detain Hamdi. That conclusion should have required an analysis of the president's claim of authority from Article II alone (and the attendant claim that such authority could be exercised in the face of a congressional prohibition). Saying that the president had only "hint[ed] of a constitutional challenge" to § 4001(a) but had not "present[ed]" one, Justice Souter "not[ed] the weakness of the Government's mixed claim of inherent, extrastatutory authority." *Id.* at 2659 (Souter, J., concurring in part, dissenting in part, and concurring in the judgment). Justice Souter argued that the president could not rely on his power as commander-in-chief to implement the traditional laws of war with respect to Hamdi, because the conditions of Hamdi's detention were inconsistent with those laws. *Id.* at 2658–59; see also *id.* at 2659 (asserting that "what I have just said about" the traditional laws of war in connection with statutory authorization "applies here [that is, to the constitutional question] as well." In addition, Justice Souter "recall[ed] Justice Jackson's observation that the President is not Commander in Chief of the country, only of the military." *Id.*

15. *Id.* at 2640.
16. *Id.*
17. *Id.* at 2641.
18. *Id.* at 2641–42. The opinion noted, "indefinite detention for the purpose of interrogation is not authorized." *Id.* at 2641.

The "perfect Constitution" assumption shows two facets in this analysis. First, the Constitution is perfect because it authorizes the president to engage in activities that the plurality concluded were appropriate for the national defense. Second, and more important, the segments of the opinions—and the qualifications each segment implicitly might place on the president's authority—show that the Constitution is perfect because, in the plurality's view, take any one segment away and Hamdi's detention might become constitutionally troubling.[19] The detention of an American citizen on the president's say-so, without congressional authorization, would be constitutionally bothersome; so would the detention, even with authorization, of a citizen seized outside the theater of war;[20] so would the indefinite detention of a citizen seized in the theater of war for purposes of interrogation;[21] and so on through each segment of the argument that the plurality opinion constructs. The "perfect Constitution" assumption underwrites the plurality's apparent nervousness about the state of affairs when one segment is cut out.[22]

As I indicated earlier, the other, seemingly more consequential aspect of the plurality opinion displays the "perfect Constitution" assumption even more dramatically. Here, the plurality adopts the standard two-stage form of constitutional analysis of questions of national power. The national government created by the Constitution is one of the enumerated powers. At the first stage, one must find out whether the national government—or, in the present context, the

19. I emphasize, though, that the plurality does not commit itself to the proposition that Hamdi's detention would be unconstitutional if one or another segment were cut out.

20. Apparently, the detention of an American citizen seized *anywhere* other than Afghanistan would be constitutionally problematic.

21. Or the detention after active combat operations end in Afghanistan of someone seized there.

22. Still, the plurality maintains a bit of distance from the "perfect Constitution" assumption because it does not formally commit itself to the proposition that the president would not have the requisite authority were one or more of the segments lacking.

president—can locate a source in the Constitution for the authority it (or he) wishes to exercise. Authority alone is not enough, though, because the Constitution also limits the powers it unquestionably confers on the organs of the national government.[23] The second stage involves asking whether some constitutional provision—in *Hamdi*, the Fifth Amendment's due process clause—limits the power the plurality concluded the president had.[24]

Justice O'Connor's reliance on the "perfect Constitution" assumption is apparent in her treatment of the due process question. Answering that question, she wrote, required the Court to balance "serious competing interests,"[25] guided by the Court's decision in *Mathews v. Eldridge*.[26] The plurality held that due process required Hamdi to be given an opportunity to challenge the government's claim that he was in fact someone who had taken up arms against the United States in Afghanistan by presenting his position to "a neu-

23. For example, no one today questions the national government's power to regulate the interstate transportation of prescription drugs by making it a crime to mislabel such drugs. However, if the government compelled a defendant to testify about her knowledge of the drug's actual composition in her own criminal trial for mislabeling, that would be a violation of the Fifth Amendment's ban on self-incrimination.

24. Justice Thomas's dissenting opinion has a passage that obscured this two-stage analysis. He began his discussion of the due process clause by raising the possibility that the clause "requires only 'that our Government must proceed according to the "law of the land"—that is, according to written constitutional and statutory provisions,'" 124 S. Ct. at 2680 (Thomas, J., dissenting) (quoting *In re Winship*, 397 U.S. 358, 382 (1970) (Black, J., dissenting)). Though rejected by the Court, Justice Black's position is analytically coherent in the context he was dealing with—that is, where the question is determining what limits the due process clause places on the power of a government of *general* power (as state governments are). In that context, Black's position gives the clause the function of ensuring that government action be authorized by constitutional or statutory provisions. That function is served by *conferring* those powers on a national government with limited powers. Justice Thomas's suggestion would make the Fifth Amendment's due process clause redundant. It is also inconsistent with long-standing precedent. See, e.g., *Murray v. Hoboken Land & Improvement Co.*, 59 U.S. (18 How.) 272 (1856).

25. *Hamdi*, 124 S. Ct. at 2646.

26. *Mathews v. Eldridge*, 424 U.S. 319 (1976).

tral decisionmaker," which could be "an appropriately authorized and properly constituted military tribunal."[27] That decision maker could rely on hearsay evidence. In addition, "the Constitution would not be offended by a presumption in favor of the Government's evidence, so long as that presumption remained a rebuttable one."[28] Thus, "once the Government puts forth credible evidence" that Hamdi was an enemy combatant, the burden could be shifted to Hamdi "to rebut that evidence with more persuasive evidence."[29]

Probably the best that can be said about these procedures is that the Court simply made them up, and its invention may not be entirely indefensible. Consider Justice O'Connor's explanation for allowing hearsay evidence to be used and for allowing a rebuttable presumption in the government's favor. She wrote that the "exigencies of the circumstances" justified those rules.[30]

As to hearsay, that explanation may sometimes make sense, at least as long as the "exigencies" are closely tied to the definition of unlawful combatant—a person seized on the battlefield—with which Justice O'Connor worked. Although the person who captured the detainee might be abroad or injured or dead, he might have provided some account of the capture to a person who could testify.[31] The difficulty, though, is that some rules against the admissibility of hearsay are predicated on the judgment that a decision maker cannot assess the credibility of a person whose story is recounted by another.

Hamdi's case illustrates the difficulty. The record before the Court in Hamdi's case was quite thin, but news accounts indicate that he was captured by the forces of the Northern Alliance, which was allied with the United States. The Northern Alliance turned

27. *Hamdi*, 124 S. Ct. at 2651.
28. *Id.* at 2649.
29. *Id.*
30. *Id.*
31. Justice O'Connor's opinion did not address the obvious next question: Does the government bear any burden of establishing the unavailability of the person whose out-of-court statements are to be admitted?

Hamdi over to U.S. forces, at which time someone affiliated with the Northern Alliance told a U.S. soldier that Hamdi had been fighting in a Taliban unit that surrendered to the Northern Alliance and, in surrendering, turned over his rifle to the Northern Alliance.[32] The legality of Hamdi's detention turns on whether the account provided by the Northern Alliance is correct; but the neutral decision maker has no basis on which to assess its truthfulness.

Now add the possibility of shifting the burden to the detainee once credible evidence against him is introduced. Again, in some contexts, such a shift might be justified. The decision maker might invoke a presumption of regularity in connection with statements made by U.S. soldiers and officials: In the absence of other evidence, the decision maker could assume that U.S. soldiers and officials tell the truth. Such a presumption would then justify shifting the burden to Hamdi to explain why their statements were not true.

Compound hearsay and the rebuttable presumption, though, and we have real problems. The presumption of regularity allows the decision maker to conclude that the Northern Alliance forces did indeed tell some U.S. soldier that Hamdi had surrendered with a Taliban unit.[33] The statement by the U.S. soldier would be credible, and—if the information about Hamdi's capture were accurate—it might justify shifting the burden to Hamdi. The real hearsay problem, though, is not with statements made by U.S. soldiers or officials; it is with the statements made *to* such officials by the Northern Alliance. Could a presumption of regularity be invoked as to those statements, the only ones that actually bear on the legality of Hamdi's detention? Justice O'Connor's opinion does not say.[34]

---

32. See *Hamdi*, 124 S. Ct. at 2637 (quoting a declaration filed in the lower courts by Michael Mobbs).

33. In addition, it allows the decision maker to conclude that that soldier did indeed tell some other U.S. official that the Northern Alliance had said so.

34. Perhaps the statement recounted by the Northern Alliance is not "credible evidence" that the detainee was an unlawful combatant. Hearsay that is inadmissible

The procedures that the plurality makes up may be fine ones—allowing a person held as an unlawful combatant a fair chance to establish that he did not actually fit into the category, while respecting the difficulties the government might face in coming up with evidence in the middle of active combat operations.[35] Or, the procedures might be quite bad ones. They might be skewed in favor of detainees if many were captured by non-U.S. forces. More likely, they might be skewed in favor of the government by allowing the decision maker to rely on hearsay evidence whose accuracy is difficult, though not impossible, to assess and then to shift the burden to the detainee—who is likely to be in a position only to tell his own story, not to come up with evidence from anyone else—to rebut the government's evidence.

As my phrasing indicates, I am skeptical about the adequacy of the procedures Justice O'Connor devised. My point, though, is not that the procedures are actually inadequate. It is that we simply cannot know whether they are—and, even more important, neither can Justice O'Connor or her colleagues. Justice Scalia called the plurality's reliance on *Mathews v. Eldridge* "constitutional improvisation."[36] A person who thought judicial balancing in constitutional law was acceptable might think that balancing works well when, but only when, the judges have had enough experience to allow them to see the advantages and disadvantages of a variety of procedures applied to a range of problems. The judges can then use a form of common-law reasoning (or, as it has come to be called, pragmatic judgment)

---

because of difficulties in assessing its accuracy might not be credible enough to justify shifting the burden from the government to the detainee.

35. Again, I think it worth noting the connection between the definition of "unlawful combatant" and the procedures the plurality found acceptable. Most obviously, the "exigencies of the circumstances" change rather dramatically once active combat operations have concluded and, in some cases, might well change significantly when the detainee was not seized on the battlefield.

36. *Hamdi*, 124 S. Ct. at 2672 (Scalia, J., dissenting).

to define the procedures that will properly balance the interests at stake in a new situation.[37]

The plurality's improvisation is troublesome precisely because the Court has essentially no experience on one side of the balance.[38] Justice O'Connor's opinion identifies the interest on Hamdi's side as "the most elemental of liberty interests—the interest in being free from physical detention"[39] and cites several cases in which the Court addressed the procedures suitable when that interest is implicated by varying statutory schemes. On the other side is the government's interest in keeping enemies off the battlefield. In designing procedures that accommodate that interest, Justice O'Connor had nothing to go on. The paragraph setting out the hearsay–rebuttable presumption rules contains not a single citation.[40] As a matter of pure theory, Justice O'Connor's opinion might have been specifying a constitutionally required minimum set of procedures, without suggesting that those procedures were the best, or even pretty good ones.[41] However, the opinion's rhetoric seems inconsistent with that theory. Even more, the Court's lack of experience with the problem at hand left it with no basis for distinguishing between minimum requirements and pretty good procedures. What Justice O'Connor did have was the "perfect Constitution" assumption: Because the Constitution is per-

37. *Cf.* Monaghan, *supra* note 1 at 374 ("perfectionists . . . analogize constitutional interpretation to the evolutionary, open-ended, case-by-case approach characteristic of the common law method of adjudication.").

38. Justice Scalia provided another, more scornful, characterization of the plurality's approach. *Hamdi*, 124 S. Ct. at 2672 (describing *Eldridge* as "a case involving . . . *the withdrawal of disability benefits!*") (ellipsis and emphasis in original). This characterization arose from his principled opposition to the kind of balancing *Eldridge* commends and need not be accepted by those who do not agree with that opposition.

39. *Id.* at 2646.

40. Nor, of course, did the justices in the plurality have relevant real-world experience with military affairs to draw on.

41. In other words, the opinion might be taken to identify the constitutionally required floor for procedures, without implying that there is no good policy reason for using more robust procedures.

fect, it *must* authorize the detention of unlawful combatants pursuant to procedures that adequately balance the competing interests.

Justice Scalia came close to seeing that the plurality relied on the "perfect Constitution" assumption, yet his perception was obscured by his obsession with judicial willfulness. He derided the plurality for its "Mr. Fix-it Mentality," the view that the Court's "mission [is] to Make Everything Come Out Right."[42] If the president failed to devise appropriate procedures, "Well, we will ourselves make that failure good, so that this dangerous fellow . . . need not be set free."[43] Further, even Justice Scalia ended up accepting the "perfect Constitution" assumption, although he "d[id] not know whether" the "tools" provided by the Constitution "are sufficient to meet the Government's security needs" because that judgment was "far beyond [his] competence . . . to determine."[44] But, in the end, he too thought that the Constitution was perfect because the courts would not intervene were the president and Congress to decide that the tools the Constitution gave them, and in particular the provision authorizing them to suspend the privilege of the writ of habeas corpus, were insufficient and therefore forged other, more effective tools that the Constitution did not really give them. In short, Justice Scalia did not himself have the "Mr. Fix-it Mentality," but he was willing to sit by and watch the president and Congress if *they* had that mentality.

Justice Scalia argued that the Constitution put the government to a choice when U.S. citizens took up arms against it: Prosecute the citizens for treason or suspend habeas corpus.[45] Criminal prosecutions come with the full set of procedures mandated by the Constitution.[46] If conditions make criminal prosecutions difficult or

42. *Hamdi*, 124 S. Ct. at 2673 (Scalia, J., dissenting).

43. *Id.*

44. *Id.*

45. As Justice Scalia's initial formulation indicates—"prosecute him in federal courts for treason or some other crime"—nothing but rhetorical force flows from focusing on treason prosecutions. *Id.* at 2660.

46. Treason prosecutions come with the special requirement that treason be

impossible, suspending the writ of habeas corpus allows the government to relax or even entirely eliminate the procedural protections available in criminal prosecutions. Those detained by the government when the writ of habeas corpus is suspended get only those procedures that Congress and the president choose to give them.

So far, so good—demonstrating, to this point, the Constitution's perfection. According to Scalia, the Constitution already provides adequate means for accommodating national security and individual liberty—at least if Congress agrees with the president that the writ should be suspended.[47] The Constitution, that is, imposes a *political* constraint on the power to meet national security needs. What if the president believes that national security requires detentions without the panoply of criminal procedure protections, and Congress disagrees, and, on reflection, we (or, as I will emphasize in the next section, the courts) conclude that the president was right? Perhaps the possibility of a dangerous political impasse can explain some uncertainty about the Constitution's perfection.[48]

More interesting, I think, are the problems associated with the suspension of the writ of habeas corpus. The Constitution appears to identify limited circumstances when Congress can suspend the writ— "when in cases of rebellion or invasion the public safety may require

---

proved by confession in open court or by testimony of two witnesses to the same act (U.S. Const., art. III, § 3, cl. 1).

47. Here I make the conventional assumption that Congress has the power to suspend the writ (or, less strongly, that presidential suspensions of the writ are permissible for only the period it takes for the president to seek congressional suspension and must terminate even if Congress fails to act one way or the other on such a request). *Cf. Hamdi*, 124 S. Ct. at 2659 (Souter, J., concurring in part, dissenting in part, and concurring in the judgment) (describing the possibility that "in a moment of genuine emergency, when the Government must act with no time for deliberation, the Executive may be able to detain a citizen if there is reason to fear he is an imminent threat to the safety of the Nation and its people").

48. Justice Scalia expressed uncertainty about the adequacy of the government's "tools" for protecting national security in a slightly different context—a discussion of detentions in connection with criminal prosecutions. *Id.* at 2673 (Scalia, J., dissenting).

it."[49] As Justice Scalia noted, one might question whether the attacks of September 11 were an "invasion" within the meaning of the Constitution and whether an invasion could then justify a suspension of habeas corpus for an extended period thereafter.[50] The Constitution would be imperfect if it prevented Congress and the president from choosing to suspend the writ merely because the framers could not anticipate all the circumstances under which suspension would be an appropriate policy response to novel forms of military attack on the United States. Justice Scalia preserved the Constitution's perfection by saying that determining whether there had been an invasion justifying suspension of the writ was a question for Congress, not for the courts.

For this proposition, Justice Scalia relied on a paragraph—really, a sentence—from Joseph Story's *Commentaries on the Constitution*: "It would seem, as the power is given to congress to suspend the writ of habeas corpus in cases of rebellion or invasion, that the right to judge, whether exigency had arisen, must exclusively belong to that body."[51] Yet, Story does not quite say what Justice Scalia needs him to say.[52] The suspension clause has two components: The writ can be suspended (1) in cases of rebellion or invasion or (2) when the public safety requires it. Story's reference to exigency reads more comfortably as a reference to the second requirement than to the first.[53] At least under modern ideas about judicial competence, it would seem easy to conclude that the courts lacked competence to deter-

49. U.S. Const., art. I, § 9, cl. 2.

50. *Hamdi*, 124 S. Ct. at 2674.

51. 3 JOSEPH STORY, COMMENTARIES ON THE CONSTITUTION OF THE UNITED STATES, § 1336 (1833), available at http://www.constitution.org/js/js_332.htm (visited Nov. 3, 2004).

52. In addition, as Jeffrey D. Jackson, "The Power to Suspend Habeas Corpus: An Answer from the Arguments Surrounding *Ex parte Merryman*" (unpublished manuscript in my possession), observed, Story provided no authority to support his conclusion, a point made by early critics of Story's view.

53. Even though Story quoted only the first requirement.

mine whether public safety required the suspension of the writ and substantially more difficult to conclude that they lacked competence to determine whether an invasion or rebellion had occurred.[54] Justice Scalia preserves the "perfect Constitution" assumption by placing outside judicial ken the possibility that Congress and the president might suspend habeas corpus when no invasion or rebellion had occurred. Or, put another way, Justice Scalia modifies the "perfect Constitution" assumption slightly: The Constitution that the courts enforce is perfect, even if the Constitution as a whole might not be.

Justice Scalia's discussion of the suspension of habeas corpus gave Justice Thomas the opportunity to express *his* agreement with the broader "perfect Constitution" assumption. Justice Thomas relied primarily on precedent to explain why detention of enemy combatants that was authorized by Congress in general and implemented by the president in good faith satisfied the requirements of due process. That approach meant that Thomas did not have to rely heavily on the kind of deep judgment embodied in the "perfect Constitution" assumption. In describing Justice Scalia's position, though, Justice Thomas wrote, "Justice Scalia apparently does not disagree that the Federal Government has all power necessary to protect the Nation,"[55] which—if, as seems to be true, this reflects Justice Thomas's view as well—is a version of the "perfect Constitution" assumption.[56] Justice Thomas's response to Justice Scalia demonstrated, in a seemingly off-

54. The most relevant cases here are *Powell v. McCormack*, 395 U.S. 486 (1969), and *Walter Nixon v. United States*, 506 U.S. 224 (1993). The former holds that the courts have the power to determine that the Constitution's reference to the "qualifications" of members of Congress refers to the three so-called standing requirements of age, citizenship, and residency. The latter holds, albeit with some ambiguity, that the courts do not have the power to determine whether impeachment proceedings pursuant to Senate rules constituted a "trial" within the meaning of the Constitution.

55. *Hamdi*, 124 S. Ct. at 2682 (Thomas, J., dissenting).

56. It should be noted as well that Justice Thomas's opinion suggests no particular concern about the possibility of an unjust detention, and to that extent, his conclusion that the Constitution authorized Hamdi's detention is at least consistent with the "perfect Constitution" assumption.

hand comment, that he did indeed share the assumption. Justice Scalia relied on Congress's power to suspend the writ of habeas corpus as a means of dealing with problems that cases like Hamdi's might present. But, Justice Thomas observed, suspending the writ "simply removes a remedy";[57] it does not make the president's actions lawful.[58] It followed, according to Justice Thomas, that Justice Scalia's position would require the president or Congress "to act unconstitutionally in order to protect the Nation."[59] And then, the "perfect Constitution" assumption comes out: "But the power to protect the Nation *must* be the power to do so lawfully."[60]

The "perfect Constitution" assumption, then, is pervasive. I turn to an analysis of its causes and then to its consequences.

II. Why Do We Assume That the Constitution Is Perfect?

The "perfect Constitution" assumption is pervasive because it alleviates several concerns. Some constitutional issues seem to require urgent resolution, but the only materials immediately at hand are the provisions of the existing Constitution. To get the problem solved,

57. *Id.* at 2683.

58. This is the traditional understanding. So, for example, an official who arrests and detains a person without probable cause while the writ is suspended is liable to the detainee for damages. See WILLIAM S. CHURCH, A TREATISE ON THE WRIT OF HABEAS CORPUS § 51 (1893). I have learned a great deal about these issues from Jackson, *supra* note 52.

59. *Hamdi*, 124 S. Ct. at 2683. Justice Thomas's analysis here might be incomplete. The suspension of the writ might bring into play *another* body of law—ordinarily referred to as martial law—under which the president's actions would be lawful. See Jackson, *supra* note 52 (citing JOEL PARKER, HABEAS CORPUS, AND MARTIAL LAW: A REVIEW OF THE OPINION OF CHIEF JUSTICE TANEY IN THE CASE OF JOHN MERRYMAN [1861]). The Supreme Court has held that the Constitution does not permit martial law to reign in areas where the ordinary civil courts are open. *Ex parte Milligan*, 71 U.S. (4 Wall.) 2 (1866). This would of course limit the possibility of the president's acting lawfully pursuant to martial law when the writ of habeas corpus had been suspended (as Justice Scalia seems to contemplate) in areas where the civil courts were open.

60. *Hamdi*, 124 S. Ct. at 2683 (emphasis added).

the Constitution *must* be perfect—and so we find ourselves forced to make the "perfect Constitution" assumption, because we believe we must solve the problem now.

We might avoid making the "perfect Constitution" assumption if we could somehow *avoid* resolving the seemingly urgent problem. However, the courts directly, and the public indirectly, will ordinarily not find it satisfactory to do so by saying, "This is indeed an important problem, which a decent Constitution would solve, but unfortunately the Constitution we have is imperfect and doesn't solve it." The reason for this is that not doing anything often will resolve the problem in line with the position taken by what we can call the *first mover*. So, for example, the president institutes a program for detaining U.S. citizens as enemy combatants, the scope of which is normatively troubling to some judges and members of the public. If the courts do nothing, the president wins—or, at least, is placed in a good position in any ensuing political struggle.[61]

Finally, and perhaps most interesting, the "perfect Constitution" assumption allows us today to place responsibility for our constitutional condition on the framers rather than on ourselves. Sometimes we might conclude that some misgivings we might have had about a particular policy were mistaken because the framers gave us a perfect Constitution. If our misgivings persist, the "perfect Constitution" assumption allows us simultaneously to blame the framers and to refrain from efforts to change the already perfect Constitution.

The role of urgency seems clear. Our constitutional system allows anyone to bring to the courts' attention constitutional problems the litigant believes to be deeply important.[62] Judges who share that belief will tend to think that they ought to do what they can to address

---

61. The president's position would be strengthened by his ability to assert correctly that the existing Constitution does not prohibit him from instituting the program.

62. Subject, of course, to justiciability concerns not relevant here.

the litigants' constitutional complaint.[63] However, all they can use is
the existing Constitution.[64] Therefore, they are likely to think that
the Constitution *must* give them the tools to address what they believe
to be an urgent problem—and, of course, to do so correctly. That,
though, is the "perfect Constitution" assumption.

The issue of what to do with so-called enemy combatants illustrates the dynamics well. Combat operations or antiterrorist investigations have placed a number of people in the government's hands.
Government officials believe that those people are bent on damaging
the nation's security; thus, the officials have to do something about,
and with, them. As a matter of both principle and political culture,
the officials will need to find some constitutional justifications for
what they end up doing.[65] To use the term that came up during the
Hamdi litigation, there are no "law-free" zones under government
control.[66] Government officials will therefore make the "perfect Constitution" assumption.

63. I describe the effects of urgency in general terms to indicate how we can
locate Monaghan's concern with substantive due process decisions in a broader context. See text accompanying note 4, *supra*.

64. The difficulty of amending the Constitution might lead to, or at least support,
the "perfect Constitution" assumption and its use of constitutional interpretation
rather than amendment, as judges and other decision makers ask, "Do you really
want us to delay resolution of this pressing problem until the cumbersome amendment process comes to its conclusion? Why shouldn't we instead act immediately
by interpreting the existing—and perfect—Constitution in a way that reaches the
right resolution?"

65. The principle is that officials of the national government, which is a government of limited and enumerated powers, have no (lawful) power to do anything for
which the Constitution does not give them authority. The U.S. political culture is
one in which all officials actually believe that they must find constitutional authority
for what they do.

66. The first use of the term "law-free zone" in connection with the government's
position that I have been able to locate is Toni Lacy, "Fates Unsure at U.S. Base in
Cuba," USA TODAY, Sept. 22, 2003. The applicable law may, of course, give executive officials unrestricted and unreviewable discretion. Yet, even in the situation
where such discretion seems most relevant—the treatment of enemies in the immediate aftermath of their seizure on the battlefield—U.S. armed forces are governed
by the laws of war. (What made the government's position in the *Hamdi* litigation

Constitutional challenges to the officials' actions ensue. What will courts do? They too are likely to make the "perfect Constitution" assumption. They must do so if they are to invalidate the officials' action because, again, the existing Constitution is the only tool they have. They are likely to do so if they uphold the officials' action for the same reasons of principle and political culture that lead the officials themselves to make the assumption.

The "perfect Constitution" assumption has another seeming advantage. It allows decision makers, particularly judges, to place, or attempt to place, responsibility for policy outcomes on the shoulders of someone—or something—else: the Constitution and its framers. Justice Anthony Kennedy's statement in the flag-burning case provides the best example of a justice coming as close as possible to saying, "It's not my fault if you don't like what we're doing." Explaining his vote to find unconstitutional a law prohibiting flag burning as a means of political protest,[67] Justice Kennedy wrote, "The hard fact is that sometimes we must make decisions we do not like. We make them because they are right, right in the sense that the law and the Constitution, as we see them, compel the result."[68]

The strategy of using the "perfect Constitution" assumption to defer criticism can sometimes be difficult to pull off. Justice Kennedy preceded his effort to do so with a sentence that undercut his point: "The outcome can be laid at no door but ours."[69] Similarly, the very

---

special was its claim that, while law in the form of the laws of war regulated the treatment of enemy soldiers, the laws of war did not regulate the treatment of enemy combatants, leaving the government with complete discretion with respect to people in that category.)

67. I believe that this is the best characterization of the Court's holding: The Court interpreted the definition of "desecration" in an antidesecration statute to identify only instances of flag destruction as a means of political protest.

68. *Texas v. Johnson*, 491 U.S. 397, 420–21 (1989) (Kennedy, J., concurring). Justice Kennedy later expressed some misgivings about having made this "hand-wringing" statement. MARK TUSHNET, A COURT DIVIDED: THE REHNQUIST COURT AND THE FUTURE OF CONSTITUTIONAL LAW 178 (2003).

69. *Johnson*, 491 U.S. at 420.

offhandedness of the plurality's construction of permissible procedures in *Hamdi* demonstrated that the decision was the justices', not the Constitution's. Still, sometimes the "perfect Constitution" assumption does work to defer responsibility—as, for example, I believe it did with respect to Justice O'Connor's treatment of the relationship between presidential power to detain and congressional authorization thereof.

So far I have suggested the attractions of the "perfect Constitution" assumption. Courts, though, can avoid the "perfect Constitution" assumption by treating the constitutional questions posed to them as nonjusticiable. They can, in form, refuse to decide whether the Constitution authorizes or prohibits the officials' action, thereby refusing to express a view on whether the Constitution is perfect. Although available in theory, this course is unlikely to be pursued by judges who believe that the problem posed is one that urgently requires resolution.

The reason is that doing nothing leaves the situation where it was when the courts were first presented with the problem, and this is not quite the status quo ante. Rather, it is the status quo after the first mover—in the present context, the president—has done something.[70] Consider a relatively pure form of the ensuing problem. The president claims that the Constitution gives him authority to do what he did, without congressional authorization or even in the face of a congressional prohibition. The litigant challenging the president's action claims that the Constitution at least requires congressional authorization for what the president did. Abstaining from deciding between those claims gives the victory to the president.

That is not quite the end of the story. A court trying to stay out of the fight might say to the litigant that her constitutional position, although perhaps correct, must be vindicated through political action

70. More generally, the first-mover advantage results from the president's position as chief executive, whose situation-specific decisions can alter the contours of the political terrain on which discussions of general policy take place.

by persuading Congress to fight the president.[71] As a matter of practical politics, though, this comes close to awarding the victory to the president—or, at least, guarantees that the political battle will be fought on grounds favorable to the president. The reason, again, is the first-mover advantage: The president has already acted. Congress must get the president to change his position, and that is likely to be difficult.[72]

To summarize: Political actors and judges find that the "perfect Constitution" assumption supports their inclinations to act in situations where they believe action is urgently required. The assumption also allows them to defer responsibility for actual outcomes to the Constitution (and its framers), avoiding the necessity to take responsibility themselves. Finally, regarding the Constitution as imperfect will relegate the problem to a political arena in which the first mover, usually the president, has a systematic advantage, notwithstanding that doing so is formally neutral as to the outcome. If these are reasons for making the "perfect Constitution" assumption (or for rejecting the alternative), what are the assumption's consequences?

III. The Consequences of Assuming That the Constitution Is Perfect

The "perfect Constitution" assumption has several consequences—some implicating the courts and the public response to their decisions, others implicating politics more broadly.

The "perfect Constitution" assumption is, again, that the Con-

71. *Cf. Goldwater v. Carter*, 444 U.S. 996 (1980) (opinion of Powell, J., concurring) (arguing that the courts should not consider the claim that the Constitution requires the Senate to participate in treaty terminations until the Senate itself as a body had asserted that claim).

72. I believe that the formal difficulties—that Congress can win its political battle with the president only by assembling the two-thirds majorities in both houses needed to override a veto—are often exaggerated. Compromises are more likely than are to-the-death combat, but the president's first-mover advantage means that the practical compromises will tend to be favorable to the position the president initially staked out.

stitution, properly construed, provides the cure for all that ails us, and, I must emphasize, sometimes it does provide an entirely satisfactory cure. We have a thick history of constitutional adjudication, providing courts with many resources to address novel problems. Often enough, those resources will lead to a decent result through a decent process. And, of course, only the "perfect Constitution" assumption allows *someone*—the courts—to try to do something to combat the executive's first-mover advantages.

The assumption's advantages are not always present, though. Suppose we discover that the disease persists or that the cure is worse than the disease was. Having moved into the mode of interpretation, we will conclude that the problem lies not in the Constitution, but in its misconstruction by the courts. In principle, of course, there is nothing particularly troublesome about a deep assumption that places the courts under close and critical scrutiny. Still, it is worth noting the irony here: The "perfect Constitution" assumption seems to empower the courts and, I believe, is strongly endorsed by those who admire the role the courts can play in our constitutional system,[73] and yet the assumption opens the courts to the kinds of sharp criticism, manifested perhaps in this chapter, that admirers of the courts typically find distasteful.[74]

An additional difficulty and another irony is that the "perfect Constitution" assumption leads to the development of incoherent and, I suggest, even anticonstitutional constitutional doctrine. Michael Stokes Paulsen's recent invocation of the "perfect Consti-

73. That proposition is one of the underpinnings of Monaghan's argument.
74. One recalls here Philip Kurland's criticism of what he saw as the Warren Court's technical incompetence, quoting the sign that supposedly appeared in bars on the frontier: "Don't shoot the piano-player. He's doing his best." Philip Kurland, *The Supreme Court, 1963 Term—Foreword: "Equal in Origin and Equal in Title to the Legislative and Executive Branches of the Government,"* 78 HARV. L. REV. 143, 176 (1964). Take the "perfect Constitution" assumption away, and the criticism takes on a different coloration: "Don't shoot the piano-player; he's doing the best that he can with badly written music."

tution" assumption in defense of what Paulsen calls "the Constitution of necessity" provides a good illustration.[75] Paulsen's thesis is this:

> [T]he Constitution should be construed to avoid constitutional implosion . . . [a]nd where such an alternative saving construction is *not* possible, the necessity of preserving the Constitution and the constitutional order as a whole requires that priority be given to the preservation of the nation whose Constitution it is, . . . even at the expense of specific constitutional provisions. Moreover, the Constitution appears to vest the primary (but nonexclusive) duty for making these sorts of constitutional judgments . . . in the President.[76]

To pin down the point: The Constitution, properly construed, gives the president the power to ignore (violate) specific constitutional provisions when, in the president's judgment, doing so is indispensably necessary to preserve the nation.[77]

Paulsen describes this as "a valuable and a dangerous arrangement"—dangerous because the power he finds in the Constitution "is capable of being misused."[78] He seeks to temper concern about misuse by describing the president's power to determine that violating the Constitution is indispensably necessary as being nonexclusive. For Paulsen, Congress and the courts have roles to play in checking the president's power: through enactment of framework legislation, control over appropriations, the power to impeach the president, adjudication of ordinary cases.[79] Yet, as Paulsen seems to understand, these checks and, even more generally, the fact that the president's

75. Paulsen, *supra* note 6. For parallel comments on Oren Gross's attempt to develop an account of procedurally constrained extraconstitutional action, see L. Michael Seidman, *The Secret Life of the Political Question Doctrine*, 37 J. MARSHALL L. REV. 441, 472–76 (2004). My criticism of Paulsen's position is entirely derived from Seidman's analysis.

76. Paulsen, *supra* note 6, at 1257–58.

77. Paulsen draws the "indispensably necessary" standard from Abraham Lincoln. See *id*. at 1290.

78. *Id*. at 1258, 1259.

79. *Id*. at 1292–93.

power under the Constitution is not exclusive, cannot truly eliminate the risk of abuse. "In the end," he wrote, "it all turns back on the office of President of the United States."[80] So, in the end, the prescription one gets from the "perfect Constitution" is, "Be very careful about who you elect as president."[81] That, however, is a deeply anticonstitutional prescription, because the point of constitutionalism is to ensure that the people's liberty will be secured by institutional arrangements, not by the personal characteristics of those holding power. Ironically, then, at least in this context, the "perfect Constitution" assumption puts the Constitution in the service of anticonstitutionalism.[82]

Another set of consequences of the "perfect Constitution" assumption involves politics. I begin at the foundation of the "perfect Constitution" assumption—the sense that specific problems urgently require resolution. That sense sometimes, even often, turns out to be mistaken. So, for example, litigation regarding the detention of enemy combatants was fueled by the sense that something needed to be done, and done quickly, to resolve the constitutional issues raised by those detentions. Yet, nothing was done for more than two years and,

80. *Id.* at 1296. To make the point obvious: Suppose the president decides that his course of action is indispensably necessary to preserve the nation and that Congress is likely to interfere with his decisions by denying him funds, attempting to impeach him, and the like. He therefore suspends the regular meeting of Congress or forcibly excludes from Congress all those he concludes are likely to vote against his program. (Similar examples could be developed for the courts.) Paulsen's "Constitution of necessity"—the Constitution, properly construed—appears to give the president this power.

81. Barry Friedman commented, in a related context, that it may be that the only solution to the normative problems associated with judicial review is, "Be very careful to pick good judges."

82. Paulsen's analysis suggests that it may not be entirely satisfactory to confine the "perfect Constitution" assumption to important matters, such as national preservation, while acknowledging the possibility of its imperfection with respect to less important ones. Doing so would mean (only) that the "perfect Constitution" assumption leads to anticonstitutional conclusions when important matters are involved, while the Constitution's imperfections regarding less important matters equally ironically *support* constitutionalist commitments.

in the case of Jose Padilla at this writing, counting. Suppose, then, that at the very outset, our instinct was not to say, "The Constitution, being perfect, resolves these problems, and all we need to do is to get the courts to construe the Constitution properly," but was instead, "The Constitution, having been written two centuries ago, is probably inadequate to the task of resolving this problem properly, so what we have to do is amend it."[83] Perhaps the public discussion of what the Constitution *should be made to say* would have yielded a better resolution, within the same two-year period, than we got from the Supreme Court.[84]

Justice Souter's opinion in *Hamdi* hinted at one way to reach this outcome, finding "one qualification" to his position that the president cannot detain a U.S. citizen without express congressional authorization: "[I]n a moment of genuine emergency, when the Government must act with no time for deliberation, the Executive may be able to detain a citizen if there is reason to fear he is an imminent threat to the safety of the Nation and its people."[85] The thought I take from this is the possibility of a system in which the president can act, subject to a requirement that the action be undone within a relatively short period, unless (in Justice Souter's version) Congress acts quickly to authorize the president's action or (in my more general version) the Constitution is amended to deal with the problem that the existing Constitution fails to deal with.

Justice Souter's opinion adopts the "perfect Constitution" assumption. It would be inconsistent of me to do so. I therefore can-

83. I note later in this chapter one obvious way in which this scenario is an impossible one.

84. I should note my sense that public deliberation in Congress over the procedures to be used to determine whether a detained citizen was in fact an enemy combatant would have generated a set of procedures that would provide somewhat more robust protection to the detainee than Justice O'Connor's opinion demanded as a minimum.

85. *Hamdi*, 124 S. Ct. at 2659 (Souter, J., concurring in part, dissenting in part, and concurring in the judgment).

not assert that the Constitution, properly construed, gives the president the power to detain for a short period, subject to some enforceable order to release the detainee if the Constitution is not in fact amended within that period.[86] In addition, the first-mover problem I discussed earlier makes it impossible to prescribe rules predicated on the "imperfect Constitution" assumption. Until we think about the ways in which the Constitution should be amended, we cannot know whether the Constitution's imperfection lies in the fact that it fails to authorize the president to take necessary actions (in which case the existing Constitution should be construed to require the immediate release of the detainees) or in the fact that it places inadequate procedural safeguards on the detention process (in which case the existing Constitution should be construed to allow the president to detain people without affording them significant procedural safeguards).

The "perfect Constitution" assumption licenses interpretations—of course, often quite contradictory ones—of the existing Constitution. The "imperfect Constitution" assumption cannot—that is its point. I suggest that the "imperfect Constitution" assumption is valuable in a different way. More than the "perfect Constitution" assumption does, the "imperfect Constitution" assumption may generate public deliberation over how a nation ordered by the Constitution should address problems quite different from those faced by the Constitution's framers. Or, to adapt Larry Kramer's formulation, We the People may do a better job of resolving our problems than They the Judges do.[87]

---

86. Were I to accept the "perfect Constitution" assumption, I would formulate the rule as one requiring release unless some significant steps were taken to amend the Constitution within a relatively short period and as requiring periodic reconsideration of continued detention in light of the progress made toward constitutional amendment. *Cf.* Bruce Ackerman, *The Emergency Constitution*, 113 YALE L.J. 1029 (2004) (proposing a system in which similar periodic reconsiderations occur).

87. For Kramer's version, see Larry Kramer, *The Supreme Court 2000 Term: Foreword: We the Court*, 115 HARV. L. REV. 4 (2001).

6. The Supreme Court and the Guantanamo Controversy

Ruth Wedgwood

IN THE CASE OF *Rasul v. Bush*, the Supreme Court decided that the statutory writ of habeas corpus should extend to the U.S. naval station in Guantanamo Bay, Cuba.[1] The petitioners, twelve Kuwaitis and two Australians captured in the course of U.S. military operations in Afghanistan, challenged the government's right to detain wartime combatants, alleging that they had not been involved with al Qaeda or the Taliban. Their status must be reexamined by a federal court, the petitioners argued, or at least by a "competent tribunal" under Article 5 of the Third Geneva Convention.[2] The petitioners did not comment on the screening procedures used by the government in the course of combatant captures and transfers, resting on the argument that only a court would do.

This was unfamiliar ground for the Supreme Court, for the capture and internment of prisoners of war and irregular combatants in overseas military operations has not generally engaged the attention of civilian judges. No American court ever sought to review the pres-

1. *Rasul v. Bush*, 124 S. Ct. at 2686 (2004).
2. Article 5, Geneva Convention Relative to the Treatment of Prisoners of War, August 12, 1949, 75 UNTS (1950) 287.

ident's procedures for capturing and interning battlefield prisoners in the Second World War, the Korean War, Vietnam, or the First Gulf War.[3] Admittedly, in those wars, it was sometimes easier to tell who was fighting for a mortal enemy.

The Court's innovation in *Rasul* also reached beyond established procedural law, for the statutory writ of habeas corpus has never been available outside U.S. sovereign territory, except in the case of U.S. citizens arrested overseas by American authorities. Without any discussion of the implications of its holding for American military operations around the world, the Court suggested that extraterritorial invocation of the federal court writ by foreign actors captured in Afghanistan was a simple corollary to a 1973 change in domestic criminal practice.[4]

It is one thing to reread a federal statute to make a housekeeping change, allocating criminal cases among federal district courts. It is rather different to say that a federal court, in the absence of any sign of congressional approval, should recast the law of remedies to issue writs worldwide. The potential hazards of this extension cannot be blinked away simply because the president or the secretary of defense is located in Washington, D.C. There has never been a U.S. District Court for Overseas Military Operations. Congress has never entertained a proposal to create such a court. Congress did create a special federal court in 1978 to regulate wiretapping against foreign officials

3. Before the war in Afghanistan, the only modern case inquiring into combatant status was the criminal prosecution of General Manuel Noriega in federal district court in Florida on narcotics charges. The former leader of Panama was captured in the course of American military operations in Panama in 1989, but was held as a criminal defendant. The government agreed to treat him as if he were a prisoner of war, without conceding that status. See *United States v. Manuel Noriega*, 808 F. Supp. 791, 794 (USDC SD FL 1992).

4. See *Rasul*, 124 S. Ct. at 2695, citing *Braden v. 30th Judicial Circuit Court of Ky.*, 410 U.S. 484 (1973). The *Braden* decision permitted a criminal defendant to challenge his state court indictment, even though he was currently incarcerated out of state, deeming him to be "in custody" in the state where the indictment was issued.

within the United States and later included physical searches as well. But Congress did not see fit to have the courts regulate U.S. intelligence operations against foreign governments or foreign persons located overseas. This long-standing fact might seem to warrant caution on the part of the courts in attempting to manage warfare through judicial writs, even in regard to the delicate issue of capturing alleged al Qaeda and Taliban combatants.

In *Rasul*, the Supreme Court did not claim its innovation was grounded in any legislative colloquy or that Congress had ever specifically contemplated allowing the writ to extend to noncitizens located in nonsovereign territory. Even the *Rasul* Court seemed to hesitate before the potentially radical consequences of the writ's extension. Abandoning its singular focus on the location of the custodian, the Court backtracked and took into account the particular location of the prisoners. The operation of the writ would not extend to Afghanistan or close to the theater of war against the Taliban, but rather only to Guantanamo Bay, an enclave under the "complete jurisdiction and control" of the United States pursuant to a lease from Cuba renewable in perpetuity.

The Court leaped before it looked. It did not stop to inquire whether there were any comparable American leases around the world. The Court did not ask whether other military bases overseas in which the United States has primary jurisdiction could fall within an extension of its new rule. The six-judge majority of the Court did show some awareness of the difficulties potentially created by its new rule, by opining that the extension of the writ of habeas corpus turned upon *both* the custodian's location in the United States and the particular status of the overseas place of internment. One of the justices who joined the majority ruling in favor of the petitioners conspicuously remarked at oral argument that Guantanamo was assumed to be unique.[5] Even so, the Court may not have fully comprehended

5. See transcript of argument, *Rasul v. Bush*, April 20, 2004 (question of Justice

how such a reading of the writ of habeas corpus could thrust the judiciary into the midst of controversies that extend far beyond the ordinary province of courts.

To be sure, the Supreme Court entertained a writ of habeas corpus in World War II to review the criminal jurisdiction of a military commission trial against a Japanese general.[6] But the trial was held by the Allied military authorities in the Philippines, when that country was not yet independent and had the status of a territorial possession of the United States. (A legal realist also might take note that the war was over, and Japan had surrendered.) In stark contrast, the Supreme Court refused to extend the writ of habeas corpus to the Landsberg prison in occupied Germany.[7] The Court turned away the plea of Germans detained by the American military in Landsberg for spying in the Chinese theater, despite the complete control and jurisdiction exercised in postwar occupation by the Allies. Supreme Court Justice Robert Jackson, former prosecutor at Nuremberg, concluded that habeas corpus could not reach to Germany and that the Geneva Conventions were not enforceable by courts. The Geneva Conventions, Jackson said, were designed to apply between countries at war, and their enforcement depended on the reciprocity of states and the vigilance of the political branches.[8] An American court, after

---

Ruth Bader Ginsburg: "I think Guantanamo, everyone agrees, is an animal—there is no other like it.")

6. *In re Yamashita*, 327 U.S. 1 (1946).

7. *Johnson v. Eisentrager*, 339 U.S. 763 (1950).

8. *Id.* at 789 n. 14 (majority opinion of Justice Jackson) ("We are not holding that these prisoners have no right which the military authorities are bound to respect. The United States, by the Geneva Convention of July 27, 1929, . . . concluded with forty-six other countries, including the German Reich, an agreement upon the treatment to be accorded captives. These prisoners claim to be and are entitled to its protection. It is, however, the obvious scheme of the Agreement that responsibility for observance and enforcement of these rights is upon political and military authorities. Rights of alien enemies are vindicated under it only through protests and intervention of protecting powers as the rights of our citizens against foreign governments are vindicated only by Presidential intervention.")

all, has no obvious power to enjoin a foreign adversary or to hold an opposing belligerent in contempt of court. But Justice Jackson's cautionary words were subject to a revised reading by the *Rasul* court, in a manner that came close to a silent overruling. In the oral argument of *Rasul*, several justices remarked that the opinion spent a good deal of time exploring the substance of issues under the Geneva Convention on the way to finding a lack of jurisdiction. Others suggested that Justice Jackson only meant to address the scope of habeas corpus grounded directly in the Constitution rather than the limits of a statutory writ.

But perhaps the most striking feature of the Court's ruling in *Rasul* is that it decides upon remedy without any serious examination of what law might be applicable. Under the habeas corpus statute, available in Title 28 of the United States code, a federal court has jurisdiction to ascertain whether a person is held "in custody in violation of the Constitution or laws or treaties of the United States."[9] Habeas is not a general writ of supervisory jurisdiction or a vehicle for ethical dismay. A writ of statutory habeas does not itself extend the substantive sources of law to an offshore jurisdiction, where the Congress or the Constitution may not intend that they reach. Nor can statutory habeas corpus sidestep the principle of separation of powers or strip the political branches of their constitutional powers in framing rules of international law. In matters of personal freedom, courts understandably feel a great inclination to intervene. But issues of war and armed conflict also depend on a framework of law that is established and enforced through political processes, both domestic and international. Both the content and effective enforcement of this law may depend upon a reciprocity that courts cannot wish into existence.

By asking about remedy before law, the Court indulged the hazard of assuming the conclusion. It would be most surprising to extend

9. 28 U.S.C. § 2241.

a remedy, at the instance of a particular party, and then to step back and conclude there was no substantive law to accompany the writ. Yet each of the possible categories of law that might be applied to overseas military operations presents particular difficulties for a court's role. This includes how international law is made through changing state practice, how courts can ascertain its content independently of the law-interpreting and law-making acts of the political branches, and whether law should be applied asymmetrically in a war with a deadly adversary.

There are four possible sources of law that might be invoked in regard to the overseas capture of belligerents: the U.S. Constitution, treaties, customary international law, and statutes. In *Rasul*, the Court did not venture that the Constitution applies to aliens captured and interned in foreign wars, even where they are held overseas under the "complete jurisdiction and control" of the United States. This may be what the Court was quietly considering without announcement. But to apply the Constitution offshore, to persons who have no connection to the United States, would be a step far beyond established precedent and certainly deserves serious analysis. To be sure, colloquy in the courtroom invoked the transcendent ideal of "due process" to be applied in ascertaining the identity of persons captured on the battlefield. One justice offered the thought that what process is "due" could be informed by the content of treaty law. But treaties do not determine constitutional arguments, and to suggest that the Fifth Amendment might in fact extend offshore to noncitizens is an extension of the Constitution that will affect a host of foreign policy interests—deserving of the most sober thought.[10]

---

10. One should note that in the case of *United States v. Verdugo-Urquidez*, Justice Kennedy offered in a concurring opinion that the search of a ranch in northern Mexico might be governed by the ultimate limits of the due process clause, where the property owner, an alien defendant, was standing trial in a U.S. federal court on narcotics charges. 494 U.S. 259, 275 (1990). That setting is rather different from a war in which the United States must prevent the ultimate harm of an adversary's threats to use weapons of mass destruction.

Nor did the justices stop to decide whether any particular treaty applied to the war in Afghanistan or the global war against al Qaeda's catastrophic terrorism. In a conventional war, the obvious sources of treaty law include the 1949 Geneva Conventions and the 1907 Hague Convention, alongside the important guarantees of the 1994 Torture Convention. The 1907 and 1949 treaties were avowedly designed for wars between organized states. Although all captured persons must be treated humanely, there is a robust debate whether the Hague and Geneva Conventions are properly applied in all their privileges and provisions to a deadly armed conflict against a private network that has eschewed the laws of war and a belligerent Afghan faction that has sheltered al Qaeda's terrorist operations. The Hague Convention has an "all participation" clause that requires all states in a war to qualify as treaty parties before the treaty can be invoked. The 1949 Geneva Conventions, including the prisoner of war privileges of the Third Geneva Convention, are limited to international armed conflict between two or more "High Contracting Parties." The mere fact that a conflict occurs on a state's territory (for example, a civil war) does not trigger the privileges of the treaty, though a floor of basic humanitarian values applies more broadly through Geneva's "common" Article 3.

There is also the challenge of how the treaty is updated in practice. The Geneva Conventions have survived for a half century because they have a "pull and tug" built into their fabric. Issues of practical application are debated in important colloquies between participating states and the International Committee of the Red Cross (ICRC) in its special role as a protective body. The ICRC does not issue private "opinion letters" like a tax agency. Yet alumni of the Red Cross movement recount that the ICRC raises issues with a state party, or passes them by, based on a pragmatic sense of what fits the situation of a particular war. It is not a simple reading of the treaty language, but rather a judgment based on state practice, what states are generally willing to accept, and what makes sense in the context of a particular conflict. In the more contentious setting of press releases and nongovernmental organization (NGO) reporting, it is sometimes hard to recall the importance of that central relationship. Certainly, a court will have little way of recapturing the flexibility that has permitted Geneva to survive as a template treaty, unless at a minimum it grants some "margin of appreciation" (an international lawyer's phrase for interpretive deference) to the state party's good-faith reading of the treaty, as informed by its colloquy with the IRC.

In the hands of an academic lawyer, for example, the Fourth Geneva Convention on the law of occupation might be read to forbid the replacement of totalitarian institutions in postwar Iraq.[11] But a monitoring agency, such as the ICRC, has instead read the convention in light of its purpose—as a safeguard against the displacement of an existing population—welcoming the construction of new democratic institutions by an occupying power that seeks to restore sovereignty to a formerly captive population. It is hard to know how a court would capture that degree of flexibility—needed in treaties intended to operate as political regimes rather than as unyielding regulatory codes.

Then there are human rights treaties, which have appropriately influenced the interpretation of the law of war. In 1992, the United States ratified the International Covenant on Civil and Political Rights.[12] The United Nations Human Rights Committee, as a treaty-monitoring body, has offered the view that the covenant *tout simple* applies to all actions of a state, including extraterritorial military operations, where any person is under the "effective control" of the state party.[13] Could the Supreme Court enforce the provisions of the cov-

---

11. David Scheffer, *Beyond Occupation Law*, 97 AM. J. INT'L L. 842 (2003).

12. International Covenant on Civil and Political Rights, Dec. 16, 1966, Art. 41, 999 UNTS 171 (entered into force Mar. 23, 1976).

13. See UN Human Rights Committee, General Comment 31, UN Doc. CCPR/C/21/Rev.1/Add. 13 (May 26, 2004); Concluding Observations of the Human Rights Committee, Israel, UN Doc. CCPR/CO/78/ISR (2003).

enant to regulate overseas military capture and internment? The answer is apparently no. The day after the decision in *Rasul*, the Supreme Court delivered its opinion in *Sosa v. Alvarez-Machain*, limiting civil damages jurisdiction under the Alien Tort Statute and barring direct enforcement of the covenant in U.S. courts. "[A]lthough the Covenant does bind the United States as a matter of international law," said the Court, "the United States ratified the Covenant on the express understanding that it was not self-executing and so did not itself create obligations enforceable in the federal courts."[14] Nor was the Supreme Court willing to conclude that every violation of the covenant should be deemed a violation of customary international law. Even apart from the Senate's reservation concerning non-self-execution, a court might hesitate to disregard the unequivocal position taken by the United States in its diplomacy that the covenant does not apply to offshore military operations regulated by the law of war. Indeed, the Senate might well have withheld its advice and consent to the treaty if the pact's domain of application was so encompassing. The covenant thus does not supply an uncontested source of law.

There is also the important body of "customary" international law—variously called "the laws and customs of war" or "international humanitarian law." It has been applied in the International Criminal Tribunals for the former Yugoslavia and Rwanda as a source of law in civil wars, where there are otherwise few applicable treaty provisions.

Customary law has two necessary elements: widespread practice by states and a general view that the practice should be legally obliging. A state can dispute and stand outside a customary law regime by protesting as a "persistent objector." If customary law is applied to a new domain (e.g., an unprecedented kind of warfare), a state might offer a similar objection.

14. *Sosa v. Alvarez-Machain*, 124 S. Ct. at 2739, 2767 (2004) (opinion of Justice Souter).

To enforce customary law under statutory habeas corpus, a federal court would first have to conclude that customary law ranks as a "law of the United States" within the meaning of the habeas statute. This is a surprisingly problematic claim. Customary international law has not been established as a basis for suit under the parallel provisions of "federal question" jurisdiction in 28 U.S. Code, section 1331.[15] In *Sosa*, the Supreme Court looked at the 1789 Alien Tort Statute (28 U.S. Code, section 1350) which provides civil recovery for "a tort . . . committed in violation of the law of nations." But even with that specific grant of jurisdiction, the Court concluded that the law of nations should be made actionable only with great caution. Justice Souter, writing for the Court, suggested that the parallel federal-question jurisdiction would likely not extend to customary law claims.[16] Though Justice Souter did not draw the point, his conclusion carries obvious consequences for customary international law claims under 28 U.S.C. 2241 as well. Justice Scalia also recalled the Supreme Court's late nineteenth-century holding that "'the general laws of war, as recognized by the law of nations' . . . involved no federal question."[17]

---

15. See 28 U.S.C. 1331 ("The district courts shall have original jurisdiction of all civil actions arising under the Constitution, laws, or treaties of the United States."). See also Andrew Baak, *The Illegitimacy of Protective Jurisdiction over Foreign Affairs*, 70 U. Chi. L. Rev. 1487 (2003); and Curtis A. Bradley, *Customary International Law and Private Rights of Action*, 1 Chi. J. Int'l. L. 421 (2000).

16. Justice Souter wrote for the *Sosa* Court as follows:

Our position *does not . . . imply* that every grant of jurisdiction to a federal court carries with it an opportunity to develop common law (so that the grant of federal-question jurisdiction would be equally as good for our purposes as § 1350 [the Alien Tort Statute]. . . . Section 1350 was enacted on the congressional understanding that courts would exercise jurisdiction by entertaining some common law claims derived from the law of nations; and *we know of no reason to think that federal-question jurisdiction was extended subject to any comparable congressional assumption.*

Sosa v. Alvarez-Machain, 124 S. Ct. at 2765, n. 19 (emphasis added).

17. See Opinion of Justice Scalia (writing also for Chief Justice Rehnquist and

The political branches have a central role in framing customary law. In *The Paquete Habana* in 1900, the Supreme Court famously wrote that customary law can be applied by the federal courts as a part of American law, but only where there are no "controlling acts" by the political branches.[18] This does not mean that courts would willingly yield to an open disregard of the law by a political branch, and the *Paquete Habana* Court did not say whether all political acts are "controlling." But the courts have credited the considered view of the political branches as to what customary law requires. One might recall the episode of the Mariel Cubans. During the Carter administration, Fidel Castro emptied his jails and dispatched the

---

Justice Thomas, concurring in part and concurring in the judgment), in *Id.* at 2770:
> The nonfederal nature of the law of nations explains this Court's holding that it lacked jurisdiction in *New York Life Ins. Co. v. Hendren*, 92 U.S. 286 (1876), where it was asked to review a state-court decision regarding "the effect, under the general public law, of a state of sectional civil war upon [a] contract of life insurance." *Ibid.* Although the case involved "the general laws of war, as recognized by the law of nations applicable to this case," *ibid.*, it involved no federal question. The Court concluded: "The case, . . . having been presented to the court below for decision upon the principles of general law alone, and *it nowhere appearing that the constitution, laws, treaties, or executive proclamations, of the United States were necessarily involved in the decision, we have no jurisdiction.*"

Id., at 287 (emphasis added).

18. As Justice Horace Gray wrote:
> International law is part of our law, and must be ascertained and administered by the courts of justice of appropriate jurisdiction, as often as questions of right depending upon it are duly presented for their determination. For this purpose, where there is no treaty, and *no controlling executive or legislative act* or judicial decision, resort must be had to the customs and usages of civilized nations; and, as evidence of these, to the works of jurists and commentators, who by years of labor, research and experience, have made themselves peculiarly well acquainted with the subjects of which they treat. Such works are resorted to by judicial tribunals, not for the speculations of their authors concerning what the law ought to be, but for trustworthy evidence of what the law really is.

Hilton v. Guyot, 159 U.S. 113, 163, 164, 214, 215.
The Paquete Habana, 175 U.S. 677, 700 (1900) (emphasis added).

sometimes violent prisoners to the United States in a Caribbean flotilla. The Court of Appeals for the Eleventh Circuit concluded that the decision of the executive branch to intern the Mariel Cubans was a controlling act that defeated any attempt to apply customary international law in favor of their release.[19] The recent decision in *Sosa* is instructive as well. *Sosa* pointed to Congress's controlling voice vis-à-vis the courts in matters of customary law. Noted the Supreme Court: The Congress "may modify or cancel any judicial decision so far as it rests on recognizing an international norm as such."[20]

In the setting of armed conflict, even the name to be given to the field of customary law is contentious. It is sometimes called "the laws and customs of war," emphasizing the central role of the practice and opinions of states. It is also called "international humanitarian law," highlighting that a formal state of war is not required for its application and connoting a relationship to human rights law. Customary law may change over time, in light of changing state practice and accepted analogies to treaty norms. There is no international legislature to adapt customary law. Rather, as commentators have often noted, a state may (in the eyes of some) seek to extend the law in order to change it. The changing nature of customary law may be one of the reasons why the valiant attempt of the ICRC to prepare a "restatement" of the customary law of armed conflict has been delayed for nearly a decade. The political branches retain a central role in determining how customary law should be modified, and when a distinctive American view of customary law should be advanced, even though other state parties may not agree. Customary law has been shaped in large part by the constitutional powers entrusted to the political branches, especially in the conduct of war. The Constitution endows Congress with the power to "define and

19. *Garcia-Mir v. Meese*, 788 F.2d 1446 (11th Cir. 1986). Compare *Clark v. Martinez*, 125 S. Ct. at 716 (2005).
20. *Sosa v. Alvarez-Machain*, 124 S. Ct. at 2765.

punish offences against the laws of nations."[21] The president is charged, as commander-in-chief, with the responsibility to conduct military operations and to punish violations of the laws of war by American troops and the adversary.[22]

There is also the challenge of "finding" the law. Much of customary military practice is captured in operational orders, rules of engagement, and military manuals, yet many countries decline to publish even their manuals. In peacetime, state practice can often be discerned only by collecting recorded incidents and demarches from the files of legal advisers' offices around the world. The published series on "United States Practice in International Law" is an important source for the American view of customary law, but few countries have a comparable recital of their state practice. *The Paquete Habana* can be read as saying that the executive's view of the content of customary law should be given controlling weight by the courts, because of this distinctive problem in "finding" the law—a problem that does not attend ordinary statutory and constitutional adjudication. The judicial caution of *Paquete Habana* also prefigures the Supreme Court's modern view of "political questions"—in some circumstances, the courts will defer because a choice has been committed to another branch or because a government cannot afford to speak with discordant voices.

Courts often rely on scholarship as a secondary source in unfamiliar areas of the law. But here too there are hazards. Few professors have diplomatic or military experience. The moral vocation undertaken by modern law schools is a worthy thing, but it can, as well, lead scholars away from a sober account of state practice to a statement of what they would like the law to be. Advocacy scholarship, from either side, cannot necessarily be relied upon for an account of the operational code of states.[23]

21. U.S. Const., Art. I, Sec. 8.
22. U.S. Const., Art. II, Sec. 2.
23. One may note the mordant view of Judge Jose Cabranes in *United States v.*

A habeas writ can also look to statutory law. Congress has been notably silent during the several years since September 11 on some of the most difficult issues. The House and Senate have approved changes to criminal law and intelligence law and provided oversight hearings after the scandalous abuse of Iraqi prisoners at Abu Ghraib. But the Congress has not attempted, as of yet, to provide a complete or "reticulated" code for the conduct of military or intelligence operations in the war against al Qaeda terrorism. The Court can look to the Uniform Code of Military Justice (UCMJ), approved by the Congress as the basis for courts-martial. But the UCMJ has a careful savings clause that recognizes and defers to the president's authority to use other forms of military tribunals, including military commissions, to exercise the nation's powers of prosecuting a war. The Congress deserves some attention, even by the Supreme Court, as an alternative source of safeguard, for even Congress's acquiescence may signal a substantive view. Checks and balances are distributed among three branches of government, and the Congress could have been asked by interested parties to extend the statutory writ of habeas corpus beyond its customary domain or to legislate on the subject of wartime captures. One question for political theorists will be whether the Supreme Court's recasting of remedies in *Rasul* has, in some measure, trenched upon the legislative and oversight role of the Congress.

In applying the Supreme Court's ruling in *Rasul*, federal courts will, at a minimum, need to be aware of their limitations in seeking to draw upon these intricate sources of law, especially in the minefield of military operations. The courts have no power to bind foreign adversaries. Courts do not fight wars and cannot issue binding orders

Yousef, 327 F.3d 56, 101–2 (2nd Cir. 2003): "Some contemporary international law scholars assert that they themselves are an authentic source of customary international law, perhaps even more relevant than the practices and acts of States. . . . [This assertion] may not be unique, but it is certainly without merit."

to al Qaeda. The contentious wartime problems of reciprocity, reprisals, and deterrence are one of the primary reasons for deference to an executive's interpretation of international law.

And then there are the desperate problems of asymmetry and perfidy. An opponent on the battlefield or in the shadows of a guerrilla war may try to take advantage of the law-mindedness of a democratic state in order to gain a fatal advantage. An opponent may use white flags of surrender with the misleading intent of surprise. Or he may force civilians to serve as shields in a battle area to prevent the other side from firing back. He may store his weapons or position his snipers in a mosque or church, holy places that are supposed to be protected in war. He may masquerade as a civilian, attempting to use the protected status of civilians as a method of surprise in the deployment of weapons of mass destruction. The cynical exploitation of humane standards—using the other side's forbearance as a way of gaining an advantage—poses a grave problem for democracies that wish to maintain moral conduct in war. In a democracy, wars are fought by citizen soldiers, whose lives are also valuable. Soldiers share the minimum claims of any human being. One reason why the Geneva tradition has conditioned some privileges upon the lawful status of a combatant is precisely to maintain an incentive system for an adversary—to persuade him to conduct warfare according to the standards of humanity.

Judges should notice as well the retrospective nature of treaty regimes, adapted to new exigencies through the interpretive practice of the executive branch. Treaties are renegotiated after a conflict is over, not while a war is on. The Western democracies have been called upon before to fit war's regulatory rules to new circumstances, by interpretation and distinction, as well as by amendment. Adapting the laws of war in the face of unprecedented challenges has depended upon sensible judgments that most often must be made by the president.

In the Second World War, for example, the trial procedures used by the Nuremberg Tribunal were in tension with the requirements of Articles 63 and 64 of the 1929 Geneva Convention on Prisoners of War. The Nuremberg trials were key in establishing the accountability of the Nazi leadership and advancing the political reconstruction of Germany. To proceed with the trials, despite the treaty, the Allies were put to argue that the unconditional surrender of a belligerent state placed its leaders in a different category from wartime captures.[24] So, too, the postwar rebuilding of Japan and Germany was arguably in tension with the rules of the 1907 Hague Convention. But the collapse of the Axis, argued the Allies, created the legal condition of *debellatio*—or total defeat—to which Hague occupation law could not apply. These lawyers' arguments were designed to advance a postwar regime that would help the world recover from a disastrous war. It is not clear, though, whether these distinctions would have enjoyed unanimous agreement among any nation's judiciary.

In the present circumstances, it is crucial to design procedures that take into account the need to protect intelligence sources, while providing a sound method of ensuring that innocent persons are not swept up in wartime operations. Though the executive branch took some time in creating a comprehensive administrative law framework, it now has in operation three separate kinds of hearings. The first are identity hearings, designed to reconfirm whether someone was involved on the battlefield as a combatant.[25] These hearings are an additional safeguard beyond prior ongoing administrative screening devices.[26] They are designed to allow a detainee to call witnesses of

24. See ANTHONY CARTER AND RICHARD SMITH, SIR GERALD FITZMAURICE AND THE WORLD CRISIS: A LEGAL ADVISER IN THE FOREIGN OFFICE, 1932–1945, at 599–609 (2000).

25. Order Establishing Combatant Status Review Tribunal, Memorandum for the Secretary of the Navy, July 7, 2004, available at http://www.defenselink.mil/news/Jul2004/d20040707review.pdf.

26. Briefing by Paul Butler, Principal Deputy Assistant Secretary of Defense for

his own, to present reasonably available information from his family and home country, to have the assistance of a military officer, and to see and confront, directly or through his representative, the government's classified information. Though they are not called Article 5 hearings under the Geneva Conventions, the three-officer tribunal would satisfy Article 5's requirement of a "competent tribunal" for the determination of an alleged combatant's involvement. The tribunals have not been invited to revisit the president's determination that al Qaeda and Taliban fighters do not qualify as lawful combatants under the Geneva Conventions. But even in a conventional war, this deference to the treaty interpretation of the commander-in-chief would be applied. One would not wish each panel of majors and colonels to offer variant readings of the same treaty. Although a lawyer is not provided for the identity hearings, the Geneva Conventions do not call for a lawyer in these circumstances.

There are also quasi parole hearings, to be held at least once a year, to determine whether a combatant is still dangerous or could safely be released.[27] Under both the Geneva Conventions and customary law, a captured combatant can be detained until the end of active hostilities. In the ongoing war against al Qaeda, it is hard to apply that standard in an ordinary way, since the war may be long in duration. Hence, the dangerousness hearings are designed to see if we can declare that a particular person's war was over, because he

Special Operations and Low Intensity Conflict, and Army Major General Geoffrey D. Miller, Commander, Joint Task Force Guantanamo, February 13, 2004, transcript available at http://www.defenselink.mil/transcripts/2004/tr20040213-0443.html. See also "Existing Procedures," described in Administrative Review Procedures for Enemy Combatants in the Control of the Department of Defense at Guantanamo Bay Naval Base, Cuba, Deputy Secretary of Defense Order OSD 06942-04 (May 11, 2004), available at http://www.defenselink.mil/news/May2004/d20040518gtmo review.pdf.

27. Administrative Review Procedures for Enemy Combatants in the Control of the Department of Defense at Guantanamo Bay Naval Base, Cuba, Deputy Secretary of Defense Order OSD 06942-04 (May 11, 2004).

has convincingly shown that he would not engage in further conflict. These hearings have sometimes resulted in false negatives—five or more persons released have reportedly returned to fighting in Afghanistan and elsewhere. Nonetheless, the intention is to mitigate the potential harshness of a war in which a nonstate terrorist network has sworn to perpetually target Americans, Christians, Jews, and dissenting Muslims, regardless of their status.

The third hearings are criminal trials before military commissions for the war crimes committed by members of al Qaeda and the Taliban.[28] The procedural safeguards of the commissions seek to preserve fundamental guarantees of the common-law system.[29] These include proof beyond a reasonable doubt, burden of proof on the government, the disclosure of exculpatory evidence, the assistance of counsel, the right to confront witnesses either directly or through counsel, the right to call defense witnesses, and the right to an appeal to a panel of distinguished judges. The appellate judges include Judge Griffin Bell, a former attorney general of the United States and former judge of the U.S. Court of Appeals for the Fifth Circuit, and William T. Coleman Jr., a former secretary of transportation in the Ford administration. The commissions' procedural rules were framed with the advice of leaders of the bar, including former Nuremberg prosecutor Bernard Meltzer and former White House counsel Lloyd Cutler.

It is worth noting that the tribunal procedures meet the requirements of Article 72 of the 1977 First Protocol Additional to the Geneva Conventions (a protocol that the United States has chosen not to ratify). As in the 1929 Geneva Convention, Article 102 of the

28. Military Order of November 13, 2001, Detention, Treatment, and Trial of Certain Non-Citizens in the War Against Terrorism, 66 F.R. 57833 (Nov. 16, 2001).

29. Military Commission Order No. 1, Procedures for Trials by Military Commissions of Certain Non-United States Citizens in the War Against Terrorism, available at http://www.defenselink.mil/news/Mar2002/d20020321ord.pdf.

1949 Geneva Convention provides that a lawful combatant should have his appeal determined by the same courts under the same procedure as a citizen soldier. But the members of al Qaeda and the Taliban are justifiably disqualified as lawful combatants, due to their organizations' consistent violation of the laws of war as well as al Qaeda's status as a nonstate terror network. It is also worth recalling that under the Uniform Code of Military Justice, even American soldiers can, theoretically, be tried under military commissions for war crimes, although as a matter of policy, courts-martial are used instead.[30]

Modern democratic states have played a key role in the development of the laws of war—both the issues of *jus ad bellum* (when war is permitted) and *jus in bello* (how war can be fought). The process of attempting to curb the harshness of war by applying rules of humanity is not a simple one. As noted above, there are treaty frameworks, but they are usually negotiated after a conflict is over to fit the last war. There is customary law, but it is a form of obliging custom that is in a constant process of change and to which states can make objections. There is a controversial category called *jus cogens*, or peremptory law, embracing a handful of norms binding on states, regardless of consent—but the membership and existence of this category has been disputed. There is the Martens clause, a natural law cousin of the Ninth Amendment of the U.S. Constitution, stating that even in the absence of an enumerated code to govern particular problems, some principles of humane conduct should apply.[31] There

30. Constitutional guarantees of due process are also directly applicable to citizen-soldiers.

31. International lawyers are less inclined to take alarm from the absence of a treaty instrument than domestic lawyers may be because of a nonpositivist view that some minimum standards must apply regardless of the absence of a written code. The Martens clause, ratified by the U.S. Senate as part of the 1907 Hague Convention IV Respecting the Laws and Customs of War on Land, 36 Stat. 2277, 1 Bevans 631—has a voice reminiscent of the American Constitution's Ninth Amendment. It

is the long-standing reluctance of states to regulate the conduct of civil wars. The customary law applicable in internal conflicts—or, in the language of the ICRC, in "internal conflicts with an international aspect"—does not embrace every feature of the treaty law applicable to international conflicts. For internal conflicts, treaty law is limited to the basic guarantees of "common" article 3 of the Geneva Conventions (the United States is a state party to this) and the sparing provisions of the 1977 Geneva Protocol II, which the United States has signed but not ratified.

In most international conflicts, the ICRC has played a crucial role as a monitor under the Geneva Conventions, substituting for the role of protecting powers and third-party states. The ICRC is granted the right of access to places of detention and, in turn, is tasked to give confidential advice to the belligerents. In a real sense, the ICRC serves as an ombudsman for the military commander, reporting news that his subordinates might prefer to ignore. It is for this reason that the U.S. government contributes one-quarter of the organization's operating expenses, and would contribute more if the organization permitted. Any historian of the ICRC will note the committee's occasional temptation to indulge in public statements of moral equivalence—in order not to alienate one particular side and lose access. In addition, in recent years, the ICRC has felt increasing pressure

---

famously reads as follows:

> Until a more complete code of the laws of war has been issued, the high contracting Parties deem it expedient to declare that, in cases not included in the Regulations adopted by them, the inhabitants and the belligerents remain under the protection and the rule of the principles of the law of nations, as they result from the usages established among civilized peoples, from the laws of humanity, and the dictates of the public conscience.

The Martens clause was meant to preclude any claim of heedless license and to ensure a minimum standard of respect for persons who are hors de combat. But it does not, as such, incorporate or anticipate every rule of the 1949 Geneva Conventions or any other domain-specific treaty.

from donors and some staff members to act in the public mode of ordinary nongovernmental organizations—using press releases and public remonstrances, rather than confidential advice. But experienced ICRC personnel recount that one important way the ICRC has adapted the law to new circumstances of warfare is by treating the treaties as a presumption but not as a procrustean bed. In the setting of trial courts and trial lawyers, this may be a harder result to achieve.

There will be times when the United States differs with the interpretations offered by the ICRC. Some ICRC staff have argued, for example, that the 1949 Geneva Conventions should be read "seamlessly" to cover all cases that could arise in wartime, leaving nothing to customary law. One contestable claim has been that a combatant who does not qualify as a prisoner of war under Geneva III must therefore be treated as a "civilian" under Geneva IV. This is lacking in common sense, since unlawful combatants would gain greater privileges through their unlawful behavior, and Sir Adam Roberts has noted the difficulty of any use of the ICRC role to extend the law beyond its domain.[32] But the point remains that the workability of

32. Sir Adam Roberts, the Montague Burton Professor of International Relations at Oxford University, has remarked upon the problem of confusion between the ICRC role of monitoring and its newer inclination to expand the law. See "The Laws of War in the War on Terror," 32 *Israel Yearbook on Human Rights* 193, 243 (2002):

> This war [in Afghanistan] occasioned a greater degree of tension between the US on the one hand, and international humanitarian and human rights bodies on the other, than any of the wars of the post-Cold War period. The handling of certain laws-of-war issues by the ICRC and various other humanitarian organisations left much to be desired. . . . [T]hey were on legally dubious ground when they pressed the US to view detainees as being entitled to be PoWs, and in their insistence that if they were not given PoW status then they must be classed as civilians. . . . Overall, the stance of such bodies, while leading to certain useful clarifications of US policy, may also have had the regrettable effect of reinforcing US concerns (well publicised in debates about the

the Geneva regime depends on an adaptive interpretation that may fall outside the "law only" powers of a domestic court.

The necessary interplay between humanitarian principles and practical experience is one reason why judge advocates general are sent into the field with military commanders to address problems in a practical way. It is why, at times, there may be some differences in view between the ICRC and national militaries—for nations must assume that the law is not always self-executing and governments are charged with the active defense of vulnerable populations. One may wonder whether the federal courts are prepared to take over this task of grit and realism, to adapt treaty principles and write rules of engagement for an unprecedented kind of war where the survival of civilians is so desperately in issue. Certainly, the province of courts in issuing a writ of statutory habeas corpus—to test whether a detention satisfies the "laws or treaties of the United States"—would not seem to authorize the Court to disregard the evolution of state practice and the law-making role of its own political branches.

Nonetheless, as a social scientist, one can see why the Supreme Court was likely to act in the setting of June 2004. Some have pointed to the Court's committed sense of relevance. Both the executive and the Congress have taken momentous decisions in the first three years after September 11, 2001. The Supreme Court had been spared any occasion to rule upon central legal issues arising from the war, and some longtime observers predicted that the justices would want to have a role. The second impetus was the justified public outcry at the abuses of Abu Ghraib and the mistreatment of a number of civilians and combatants detained in the Iraqi war. News stories about

---

International Criminal Court) about zealous international lawyers standing in unsympathetic judgement of the actions of US forces.

See also Adam Roberts, "What Is a Military Occupation?" 55 *British Yearbook on International Law*, 249, 302 (1984) ("Both the ICRC and the United Nations have on numerous occasions asserted the applicability of international humanitarian law to particular situations, irrespective of the issue as to whether they count as international armed conflicts and/or occupations.").

the events in Iraq and concern about any possible similar practices at Guantanamo framed the public mood while the Court drafted its opinions. The Congress and the military undertook investigations, which are still ongoing, and the uniformed military has shown a willingness to discipline its own ranks. The Supreme Court has no modern practice of holding cases over until a following term and, thus, could not see how the matter unfolded in the remedial response of the other two branches of government.

The third influence on the Court was the disclosure of Office of Legal Counsel memos that took an unwarranted view of executive power. It is one thing to debate the extent to which the law of war is justiciable. It is another matter entirely for a government lawyer to inform the executive that there are no limits at all that deserve attention—whether in treaty law, customary law, human rights standards, or the core commitments of the Martens clause. In February 2002, President Bush publicly committed the United States to the humane treatment of all persons captured in the war on terrorism, including members of al Qaeda and the Taliban.[33] The president also pledged the application of the principles of Geneva wherever possible in the fight against al Qaeda.[34] But an August 2002 memo of the Office of the Legal Counsel[35] took a casual and distorted view of the applicable standards of the Torture Convention and has now been officially rescinded. The memos certainly gave decision makers an incomplete account of the law and did not report variant legal views taken by other departments and other governments.[36] The Supreme Court may have felt impelled to step in, to reassert that there is some law

33. Ari Fleischer, White House Spokesman, Special White House Announcement Re: Application of Geneva Conventions in Afghanistan, Feb. 7, 2002, at LEXIS, Legis Library, Fednew File.

34. Id.

35. Standards of Conduct for Interrogation under 18 U.S.C. 2340–2340A, Memorandum for Alberto R. Gonzales, Counsel to the President, Aug. 1, 2002.

36. See Ruth Wedgwood and James Woolsey, Law and Torture, WALL ST. J., June 28, 2004.

applicable to our conduct abroad, even if it should fall within executive competence.[37]

Mr. Dooley once observed that the Supreme Court follows the election returns.[38] In a modern age of media, it is a rare judge who can abstain from reaction to public concerns or an immediate moral crisis. The psychological posture of a judge, as Jerome Frank might have remarked, is inevitably influenced by the public conversation. The divisions in American society, and criticism from Europe, unsurprisingly might have an effect on human judges.

But one of the cautions against an overambitious theory of jurisdiction is precisely the fact that on some issues there may be no settled rules to apply. This is not a nihilistic claim of lawless space — indeed, the imprudent and dismaying argument that there are no legal principles that should ever constrain American power is precisely the point of view that tempts a court to act. But the federal courts have never taken the primary role in developing the law of armed conflict, and no developed body of rules fits all the dilemmas of this new type of warfare. The Swiss government, as depository of the Geneva Conventions, has implicitly acknowledged this problem, convening several conferences to discuss whether to seek a new treaty instrument for the war against catastrophic terrorism.

In creating a limited remedy to address the question of mistaken identity, the Court has not blockaded the laws of war. In the companion case of a Saudi-American citizen, Yaser Hamdi, Justice O'Connor offered a plurality opinion suggesting that questions of combatant identity can be ascertained through the procedures of military tribunals, including the use of hearsay evidence.[39] But the Court should stop and think before considering further predictable pleas to assume control of the many other complicated questions of military captures, including the qualification of unlawful combatants and the

37. Compare the views of Justice Jackson, supra note 8.
38. FINLEY P. DUNNE, MR. DOOLEY'S OPINIONS 26 (1901).
39. *Hamdi v. Rumsfeld*, 124 S. Ct. at 2633 (2004).

release of persons found to be no longer dangerous. The role of Guantanamo as an offshore operating base in overseas refugee crises also might be of passing interest to judges in recasting the scope of a remedial writ.

The Supreme Court may be inclined to maintain a type of "strategic ambiguity" on questions of review, in order to summon the executive branch and Congress to appropriate moral attention. But a judge should hesitate, and hesitate again, before assuming the conduct of a war in some new form of "managerial judging." Mindful of America's historic concern about fairness to all individuals and commitment to procedural regularity, a judge must also acknowledge a democratic government's abiding duty to protect civilians from catastrophic harm at the hands of a ruthless adversary. Ultimately, the propriety of American government and our country's conduct in the world depend upon the alertness of a democracy and the attention of its electors, as well as the quality of its judges.

Contributors

PETER BERKOWITZ teaches at George Mason University School of Law and is a fellow at the Hoover Institution, Stanford University. He is cofounder and director of the Israel Program on Constitutional Government and served as a senior consultant to the President's Council on Bioethics. He is the author of *Virtue and the Making of Modern Liberalism* (Princeton University Press) and *Nietzsche: The Ethics of an Immoralist* (Harvard University Press), as well as editor of the companion volumes *Varieties of Conservatism in America* (Hoover Institution Press) and *Varieties of Progressivism in America* (Hoover Institution Press), and of *Never a Matter of Indifference: Sustaining Virtue in a Free Republic* (Hoover Institution Press). He has written on a variety of topics for a variety of publications.

MARK TUSHNET is Carmack Waterhouse Professor of Constitutional Law at the Georgetown University Law Center. He is the coauthor of four casebooks, including the most widely used casebook on constitutional law; has written twelve books, including a two-volume work on the life of Justice Thurgood Marshall, and has edited four others. He was president of the Association of American Law Schools in 2003. In 2002, he was elected a fellow of the American Academy of Arts and Sciences.

PATRICIA M. WALD is the former chief judge of the U.S. Court of Appeals for the D.C. Circuit and served as a judge on that court from 1979 to 1999. She was then the American judge on the International Criminal Tribunal for the former Yugoslavia from 1999 to 2001. She is a graduate of Yale Law School and is currently a member of the President's Commission on the Intelligence Capabilities of the United States Regarding Weapons of Mass Destruction.

SETH P. WAXMAN, former solicitor general of the United States, is a partner at the law firm of Wilmer, Cutler, Pickering, Hale and Dorr; a member of the faculty at the Georgetown University Law Center; and chair of *Legal Affairs* magazine.

RUTH WEDGWOOD is the Edward Burling Professor of International Law and Diplomacy at Johns Hopkins University and a member of the board of editors of the *American Journal of International Law*. She is a member of the Secretary of State's Advisory Committee on International Law, the Defense Policy Board, and the CIA Historical Review Panel, and she served as the Charles Stockton Professor of International Law at the U.S. Naval War College. She is also the U.S. member of the United States Human Rights Committee.

BENJAMIN WITTES is a member of the *Washington Post* editorial page staff. He is the author of *Starr: A Reassessment* (Yale University Press) and is a regular contributor to the *Atlantic*.

JOHN YOO received his bachelor's degree, summa cum laude, in American history from Harvard University. He received his J.D. from Yale Law School, where he was an articles editor of the *Yale Law Journal*. He clerked for Judge Laurence H. Silberman of the U.S. Court of Appeals for the D.C. Circuit. Professor Yoo joined the Boalt faculty in 1993, and then clerked for Justice Clarence Thomas of the U.S. Supreme Court. He served as general counsel of the U.S. Senate Judiciary Committee from 1995 to 1996. From 2001 to 2003, he served as a deputy assistant attorney general in the Office of Legal Counsel at the U.S. Department of Justice, where he worked on issues involving foreign affairs, national security and the separation of powers.

Index